ORGANIZE YOUR JOB SEARCH!

ORGANIZE YOUR JOB SEARCH!

SIMPLE SOLUTIONS FOR FINDING THE JOB YOU WANT

RONNI EISENBERG WITH KATE KELLY

HYPERION

NEW YORK

Library of Congress Cataloging-in-Publication Data

Eisenberg, Ronni.
Organize your job search : simple solutions for finding the job you want / Ronni Eisenberg with Kate Kelly.
p.   cm.
ISBN 0-7868-8467-3
1. Job hunting–United States–Handbooks, manuals, etc.
I. Kelly, Kate. II. Title
HF5382.75.U6E57 2000
650.14–dc21   99-17003
                                                      CIP

First Edition

3   5   7   9   10   8   6   4   2

Design by Robert Bull Design

CONTENTS

INTRODUCTION

Everyone who is thinking about looking for a new job or changing careers says the same thing: Getting started is the hard part. That's why *Organize Your Job Search!* starts at the very beginning and breaks the entire process down into simple steps to get the job search underway.

As you continue through the book, you'll find easy, straightforward advice for all aspects of the search and a complete plan for landing a great job. There are tips on everything from writing a first-rate resumé and performing well on an interview to staying in control of the process. The end result will be a job you want and a new set of organizational skills—not a bad combination at all.

HOW TO USE THIS BOOK

You can approach the book in two ways. If you're the type of person who likes to get an overview before starting a project, then read the book straight through so that you have an idea of where you're going. Then go back and follow the steps you need to organize your search.

If the big picture overwhelms you, then take the information one step at a time. As you read about the Job Search Notebook, stop and create it right then. When the discussion turns to goal setting, take the time to work through the process carefully. Just be certain to stay on track with finishing the book and preparing your materials. At the conclusion of the book, your job search will be well underway.

MAKE THE COMMITMENT

Set a "job-hunting" schedule for yourself, and use the "to do" list in the back of the book to stay focused.

> ## "TO DO" ITEM #1:
> **I will finish this book by_____.**
> **(See below for suggestions on setting a date.)**

If you expect to read the book straight through, then the date given above should be no later than a week from today. As you'll soon see, the reading will go quickly. Within each chapter you'll have the opportunity to set interim deadlines for completion of specific steps on the way to the job that's right for you.

If you plan to work through each step as you read, then the date you set for finishing the book should be no longer than a month from today. If you take any longer, then the enthusiasm (or need) that drew you to buy this book will subside, and you'll be back where you started, overwhelmed and uncertain about when you're going to get around to finding that new job.

If you remain organized as you go through the job search, I guarantee you that the calm and control that you'll feel will radiate to your job interviews, and first thing you know, you'll have the job offer you want.

Organized people are determined people, and determined people get ahead, so let's get started.

PART ONE

GETTING STARTED

1

GETTING STARTED

WHAT'S AHEAD

Commit the Time
Make an Appointment with Yourself

Getting started. It's not easy. Even if the subject at hand wasn't "new job," "different job," or "first job," it's still hard to undertake a new project. Whenever we're faced with something unfamiliar, it's intimidating: *How will I know what to do? What if people laugh at me? What if I do the wrong thing? What if no one likes me? What if I fail?*

So how do people take on a new project or start something new, like looking for a new job? **They get organized.**

When it comes to organizing something like a job search, the process involves gathering the materials you'll need and then breaking the entire process down into small, manageable steps—steps you can do while continuing to live your regular life—whether you're already working, still in school, or prepared to devote full-time to looking for a job.

The person who gets organized is best prepared to run an effective job search because he or she:

— Sets specific goals based on a current situation and long-term interests;

— Makes a plan for the search—an absolute necessity in landing a job;

— Prepares accurate, carefully considered resumés and cover/pitch letters that are tailored to each situation;

— Keeps careful records of the people who can help;

— Can always locate the information (brochures, notes, reports, papers) about a company or a person needed for the search;

— Stays on top of the search by following up regularly with active leads—

and that's what lands a job.

Because the search is broken into parts—and because I'll teach you a system for keeping track of everything you need—you'll find a key benefit to this process: **You'll be able to maintain momentum,** a vital part of mastering anything new.

So if you were feeling like you don't know where to begin, like you'll never know where to begin, and as if at this point, you'd just as soon not begin at all—relax. This book is going to take care of everything for you.

COMMIT THE TIME

While it's impossible to set a date by which you'll have your new job, what you can do is plan out an approximate timetable for when you would like to have that job in hand. This, in turn, will tell you how to schedule yourself right now.

If you're a student, you have a graduation date, so you have a good idea of the time when you'd like to have a job; if you're currently unemployed or in a job you loathe, then your timetable is "the sooner the better." For those of you who are currently in jobs that are "okay," then your situation may be less urgent. However, if you don't get going, you're just procrastinating—you might as well start now.

Looking for a job is a job in itself. The more urgent your need or desire, then the more time you should set aside for your search. If you're not burdened by working, then plan to devote 20–25 hours per week to running your job search.

If you're hoping to change jobs in the next 3–9 months, then you can afford to go through the process a little more slowly, though I still recommend that you plan to devote some time to your job search **every single day.** It will be easier if you make it routine.

MAKE AN APPOINTMENT WITH YOURSELF

- Use your calendar or day planner to write down a specific time at which you plan to work on looking for a job.

- If you are unemployed, then the search is your full-time job. Get up, get dressed, have breakfast, and establish a time when you plan to start work.

- If you're a student, take a look at your class schedule, and then block out time each day when you can work for a while uninterrupted.

- If you already have a job, you'll need to be a little more flexible. Schedule time for before or after work for writing letters or sending out resumés. On days when you need to make phone calls (a big part of looking for a job), you're going to have to evaluate the following. Considering my current position, should I:

— Arrange to come in an hour late one or two days per week?

— Arrange to leave an hour early one or two days per week?

— Find a way to take my lunch hour at a time when I can do some phoning?

• If you're employed, you may have to take some days off for interviewing, so keep this in mind when you consider taking any personal time off—you don't want to appear to be sloughing off at your current job.

"TO DO" ITEM #2:

On your calendar, block out time daily to devote to your job search.

By blocking out time on your calendar, you've made an appointment with yourself that will not only preserve the time for this priority, but it will also help provide the discipline to get it done. That time on your calendar should be taken as seriously as you would a dental appointment or a lunch date with a good friend.

In the next chapter you'll learn how to organize everything you need for your job search—and the nice thing is, you've already established when you're going to do it!

KEEP IT SIMPLE

1. Finding a new job means devoting time to the search. If you need a job immediately, then plan to spend 20–25 hours per week on your job hunt; if your need is less urgent, you should spend no less than five hours per week working toward your goal.

2. Block out specific time for tasks devoted to getting a new job.

3. If you're currently employed, you may need to take days off now and then in order to go on interviews and do a lot of the necessary phoning.

2
YOUR JOB SEARCH TOOLS

WHAT'S AHEAD

Looking for a job is much easier if you have the systems and the items you need at your fingertips.

— When a potential employer says, "Call me next week," you need to have a method for keeping track of his name and phone number as well as a way to remind yourself to call on the appointed day.

— When a company is hiring and the person you speak to says, "Send me your resumé," you want to have one ready to go.

— When that "ideal" company decides that you're the one for the job, you want to be certain that when they phone you get the message.

Without preparation and organization, all your hard work could be wasted. The next two chapters are going to tell you what you need to know about the supplies, equipment, and services that will be important in your job hunt. This chapter focuses on purchasing the basic supplies and establishes systems for keeping track of all the information you'll gather during the job search. The next chapter discusses setting up your headquarters.

A SHOPPING LIST OF SUPPLIES

The first thing to do to get ready for a job hunt is to purchase the supplies you'll need in the coming weeks:

- stationery, including envelopes and business cards;
- day planner or calendar system;
- a three-ring looseleaf notebook (for creating a Job Search Notebook, which is explained later in this chapter);
- dividers with pockets;
- three-hole paper for the binder;
- a file drawer or file box;
- file folders:
  - twelve file folders of one color;
  - thirty-one of another (for creating action files, described later in this chapter);
  - fifty ivory-colored file folders for keeping brochures, employment booklets, and press releases about a company all in one place.
- a Rolodex;
- business card holder;
- message board.
- It's also helpful to have telephone books for the communities in which you're job hunting. Call your local telephone company about ordering them. Allow 2–3 weeks for delivery.

Business Stationery

Not that long ago, job hunters were expected to invest in quality stationery in order to launch a serious hunt. Today with the attractive designs that can be created on home PCs, this investment is no longer necessary. "It's more about what the letter says, and less about how it looks—so long as it's neat," says one executive.

If you plan to design your letterhead yourself:

- Organize your design for clarity. Make certain your name, address, e-mail address, and telephone number are easy to read and easy to find on your letterhead design.

- Purchase better quality laser paper for your cover letters and resumé.

- Stop at a quick printer and select good quality #10 business envelopes (select something that comes close to matching the paper you're planning to use), and have your return address printed on them. This needn't be a big expense, and the print job can be done in a matter of days. Having a professional-looking envelope will make a difference in how your overall package appears.

"TO DO" ITEM #3:

Select a good quality copier paper and order personalized envelopes to match.

- Invest in business cards. While you're getting your envelopes printed, get some attractive business cards printed as well. There is no substitute for being able to hand a new contact a small card with your name, e-mail address, address, and phone number on it.

"TO DO" ITEM #4:

Order business cards.

SELECT A CALENDAR SYSTEM TO STAY ON SCHEDULE

- Use one calendar system or day planner as your basic scheduling tool. A paper-based planner, a calendar program on your computer, or a palmtop computer are among your options. With any method you choose, be certain of three things:

1. The style you choose should have plenty of space for noting appointments. (Keep this in mind, especially, if considering a pocket calendar.) Because you will be visiting many different, unfamiliar locations for interviews, you'll want to write down complete addresses as well as phone numbers for all appointments.

2. There should also be space for a daily "to do" list.

3. You should be comfortable using it.

- Develop the habit of writing **everything** down. The last thing you want to do is forget about an interview or lose an important telephone number.

"TO DO" ITEM #5:

Select a good calendar system with enough space for writing out appointment information and keeping a daily "to do" list.

CREATE A JOB SEARCH NOTEBOOK

Divide the notebook into the following sections by labeling the dividers accordingly:

- **Your Master List**
  This is where you'll keep a running list of everything you have to do in your pursuit of a new job. (This is explained more fully later in the chapter.)

- **Career Goals**

  This section is for recording your thoughts regarding what type of job you want or could do. Long-term career planning ideas should be a part of this section.

- **People**

  List all the people whom you should contact to help with your search.

- **Places**

  Also write down names of helpful organizations and target companies (those likely to have the type of job you're seeking.)

- **Letters Sent**

  Store copies of all the letters you send out in this section. File them in alphabetical order by contact's name for easy retrieval. On the back of the letters you can keep notes regarding subsequent conversations and meetings.

- **Interview Preparations**

  This section will include some general questions (and your thoughts on the best answers) for which you will want to be prepared, as well as a list of questions you want to ask about each job. (All this is more fully explained later in the book.)

- **Follow Up**

  Keep a thank-you note list and check it off after you've written to someone. Once you've been interviewed at a company, letters and related material should be moved here. This will provide an organized method for following up.

ACTION FILES

Q: How do you remember what to do when?

A: You create "action files."

While handheld computers, regular computer programs, and personal digital assistants all have terrific "reminder" methods that you're welcome to use, there's still no substitute for a paper-based reminder system. It's an ideal way to be sure you follow up with the right people at the right time—an absolute necessity when pursuing a new job. Here's how to create a terrific Action File system for pending items:

- **What you need**: A total of 43 folders—one for each month of the year to hold long-range items, and 31 for each day of the month, for short-range details. Select one color for the monthly folders and another color for the daily files. Label 12 by month, and number the rest, 1–31.

- **What you do**: If it's March 30, and you want to date-file a letter that requires follow-up on April 12, place the letter in the folder marked "12." Or if you plan to wait until May to follow up, then the letter should be placed in the "May" file. On May 1, pull that month's folder and sort through it. Place all those papers into files that correspond with the appropriate dates.

This system guarantees follow-up. When someone tells you, "I don't know if that job is going to open up, but call me in a month," you will be one of the few job seekers who has a system for following up as suggested. It definitely can make the difference between getting the job and not getting the job.

"TO DO" ITEM #7:
Create a set of "Action" files for follow-up.

YOUR MASTER "TO DO" LIST

A Master "To Do" List takes the stress out of having to remember everything. You'll also find that it keeps you focused and provides direction for each day of your job search. It also offers the following additional benefits:

— A Master "To Do" List replaces all those little scraps of paper people use to write things down. You're now going to keep everything on one list in the front of your Job Search Notebook.

— Everything you need or want to do as part of your job search is collected neatly in one place.

— Your Master "To Do" List provides you with a running list of tasks from which to build your daily "to do" list.

• On the left side of the page note the date of the entry; on the right side, note the task's deadline. As you write down things to do and phone calls to make, you'll begin to create a "history" of your job search. Because tasks are recorded by date, even miscellaneous items are easy enough to find again.

• Always note in your Master "To Do" List the basics of the information you need. If you're to call someone, note the telephone number; if you're to mail them something, write down the address.

• From this point on, write down all the "to do" items that are highlighted in this book.

• Use your Master "To Do" List as a "jotter." When you're on the phone and a contact is giving you names and phone numbers of people whom you should approach, note all the information on your Master "To Do" List.

• Add to that list all the ideas you have for mounting your particular job search. Whenever you think of a new person to contact, a new company to check out, or a new idea to explore, write it on this Master "To Do" List. Get in the habit of writing *everything* down—from "buy stamps" to "call Ken about possible opening at his company." Review your goal sheets weekly (these are the lists of what you hope to accomplish, and they are explained in Chapter 5), selecting a reasonable number of tasks to undertake during each upcoming week.

- If a task seems overwhelming, break it into small parts. If you plan to apply to graduate school to become a psychologist, you need to outline specific steps to take. Some of them will be:

  — Call graduate program in area for information on what testing is required for applicants;

  — Register for appropriate tests;

  — Review for tests;

  — Visit library to investigate schools;

  — Call or e-mail for brochures and applications from schools that seem appealing. The list should continue in this way.

- As you can see, the tasks themselves vary from a single phone call to some library research, but no single item is overwhelming when it's broken down into these parts.

- Set priorities so that you can focus on the most important tasks first.

- Set realistic deadlines for various steps on the way to your goals. (With some of the "to do" items in *Organize Your Job Search!* you have been asked to fill in deadlines.) There's something about a due date that makes the task much more important, and with a self-motivated project like job hunting, you really need to establish ways to stay on schedule.

- In all my other books, I recommend rewards for meeting deadlines, and it's all the more important here. Establish mini-rewards (a new paperback book? meeting a friend at your favorite coffee bar?) for reaching certain milestones like finishing your resumé or setting up your first interview.

- All papers related to items on your Master "To Do" List belong in appropriate files—not stacked around the room. Use the file folders you purchased, and store the files in the file box or file drawer.

PREPARING YOUR DAILY "TO DO" LIST

- Set aside ten minutes at the end of each day to prepare a "to do" list for the next day.

- Review your Master "To Do" List, deciding what tasks should be undertaken the next day. Write these items on your "to do" list to create your plan for the next day.

- Note any undone items from that day's list and carry them over if necessary. Cross off the items you have finished.

- Add any new tasks that you think of that can be accomplished.

- On your daily "to do" list, place asterisks by the priority items so that you know what you **need** to do if you're in a time crunch.

KEEPING TRACK OF INFORMATION

After you've created your next day's "to do" list, there are one or two other things to do:

- Transfer the "history" of your day into the notebook. If you followed up with Company XYZ to whom you'd written a week ago, start a log of this experience on the back of the copy of the letter you sent. Note the secretary's name, the day you called, what developed out of the phone call, other people at the company with whom you've spoken, etc.

- Turn to the "People" section in your Job Search Notebook.

- Transfer any names and phone numbers of people you've written on your Master "To Do" List with whom you'll want to follow up. (You can also do this on your Rolodex.)

SPECIAL ADVICE

- If your Master "To Do" List notes: "Follow up with T. Jones regarding the job opening," and you've learned that he's away for a week, maintain control of the situation. Don't leave a message. Skip forward in your calendar to the following week, and make a note to call again. Keep phoning (and using this reminder system) until you make contact.

- Keep pen and paper in logical places so that you're sure to write down ideas (new people to contact, new companies to investigate) when you think of them: by your bedside; in your car (purchase an "autopad" with pencil attached); by all telephones; in your brief-case. Make notes when you think of them and then add them to your Master "To Do" List once you're home again.

- Leave messages for yourself on voice mail if you're away and are afraid you'll forget.

RECURRING "TO DO" ITEM: READING

The successful job seeker is someone who is well-rounded and makes it a point to stay current. Here's how:

- Read your daily newspaper every day (and do so before any inter-view, no matter how early you have to get up). If you're interview-ing out of town, make it a point to read that town or area's newspaper online for a week or two prior to your interview. In ad-dition to providing you with ideas for "small talk," it keeps you abreast of what's going on locally, which may affect the business to which you're applying.

- If you're looking for a career in business, read *The Wall Street Journal* and *USA Today* every day. Most business people do, and you don't want to be saying, "Whaaaat?" if your interviewer should refer to something in that day's paper. Also stay current with major business publications like *Forbes, BusinessWeek*, and *Fortune*.

- Find out what the important trade publications are in your chosen field, and take out a subscription, or get to the library to read it regularly.

- Check your area for regional business publications that might be of value.

- How to keep up with all this reading? Learn the art of scanning for information. If you're applying for a job in retail management, you can skip articles pertaining to the paper industry, the banking industry, and many others.

- As you read, make note of names and titles of people in companies that interest you. While "blind" approaches are a long shot, an intelligent letter from you about a recent article in which someone was quoted may well get you the meeting you want.

KEEP IT SIMPLE

1. **A calendar, your notebook, action files, and a "to do" list are your essential tools for your job search.**

2. **Create a running Master "To Do" List filled with all your job search ideas.** Then create a realistic daily "to do" list, culled from your Master List.

3. **Add one recurring item to each daily "to do" list: reading.** Stay current on both local and industry news.

3

SETTING UP
JOB-HUNT
HEADQUARTERS

WHAT'S AHEAD

Establishing Your Headquarters
The Telephone
Using a Cellular Phone
Using a Pager
Using an Answering Machine
Arranging for Faxes

While there's no need to set up a full-scale home office in order to start your job search, there are certain elements of an office that are very important to staying organized. At the very least, you need a quiet place to work where you can also keep everything all together. You must also establish viable ways for people to reach you—whether it's by phone, by pager, e-mail, or by fax.

Thanks to the invention of cell phones, I know one fellow who ran his entire job search from his car—he told me his backseat was his "office" and his trunk was his "file cabinet." While he did eventually get a good job, his life would have been less frantic if he'd devised ways to keep all his paperwork organized.

Here's what you should do:

ESTABLISHING YOUR HEADQUARTERS

You will need a headquarters of some type where you can keep everything related to this project. That way no one will misplace your papers or rearrange your files—you'll know exactly where everything is.

- If you have an extra room in your home that can be used, this is ideal. It provides you with the quiet and privacy for making telephone calls and gives you a specific place to store your materials.

- If you don't have a room, do you have a desk you can use? If you can, move the desk to a quieter part of the house so that you can work uninterrupted.

- Office supply catalogs sell rolling storage units, and storing everything in one of these gives you a handy way to bring everything out when you need to.

- If none of the above options are workable, then clear out a closet shelf or a bookshelf where you can keep everything related to your job search. The important thing is to keep all of your materials together where you can find them.

THE TELEPHONE

The telephone will eventually link you to your next job. You'll undoubtedly make countless outgoing calls throughout the process, and the incoming calls may contain good news of an interview scheduled or a job to be had. For that reason, the following is important:

— Callers should be able to leave a message if you're not in.

— Callers should not get a busy signal.

— Callers should be able to reach you or hear back from you within one to two hours of their call.

— Callers should not hear household or roommate chaos.

Some job seekers establish rules for use of a home telephone line; others are benefiting from new technology and are using cell phones and pagers to receive calls and/or messages. Here are some tips for each:

Using a Home or Apartment Telephone

- If the telephone belongs solely to you, then:

  — Get an answering machine or sign up for a voice mail service to cover your telephone when you're not there. (Caller ID is not helpful at this time; you need to know exactly who called and what message they wanted to leave.)

  — If you opt for a machine, be certain that you can retrieve messages without going home.

  — You can prevent having callers get a busy signal by signing up for Call Waiting or a voice mail service. With Call Waiting, you're beeped midcall, signaling that you need to check to see who else is calling; with voice mail, you also hear a beep but the voice mail system will record a message if you don't pick up right away.

  — If you have roommates, loud pets, or children, a telephone with a "mute" button lets you control outgoing sounds from your household, presenting a more professional image.

  — Call Forwarding allows you to leave your "headquarters" and still receive all your messages. If you have a car phone or a current job where you answer your own phone, you may want to have calls forwarded so that you can receive them more quickly than if you have to phone in for messages.

- If others also use the telephone, you need to talk to them about your job hunt. Whether it's giving specific instructions about messages to your teenager, talking to your toddler about not picking up the telephone, or asking your college roommates for cooperation, it's important to convey to them how very important it is that you get *all* messages.

- Ask that all messages be taken politely and carefully. Explain to others that during this period, "Bob called" means nothing to you. You need a full message: "Bob Smith, XYZ Company, please return his call: 555–3214"

- Set up a message board by the primary telephone.

  — Use the board to post any significant information about your own schedule: "Out until noon; I'll return all calls this afternoon," or "Gone all day; I'll call in for messages by 2:00 P.M."

  — Take responsibility for providing paper and pen (attach it with string to the board so it won't disappear) to assure that there's an available writing implement for taking messages.

  — If a message might be taken for you on any of several telephones, provide message pads and pens for each location. Designate a central location where everyone's messages—including yours—are left.

USING A CELLULAR PHONE

If you're out and about a great deal, you may decide that a cellular phone makes more sense. There are two basic types to consider:

People who are in their cars a great deal often opt for a car phone. These can be installed in your car and purchased with features such as voice-activated dialing and speakerphone connections that aid in safer driving while talking. (Recent studies indicate that any type of telephone use while driving increases accident risk.)

Other cellular phones are the kind that fit into your purse or breast pocket, and they range from serving as a simple telephone to being your full-service connection with the world. Some recent models have a small display that enables you to read e-mail, check appointments, play back voice mail messages, and even play games when you're bored.

- If you don't already have a cell phone, visit a telephone store and select the model that has the features you need.

- Ask about battery performance—talk life vs. standby life. You also want a low-charge alert function so you don't miss calls because your batteries suddenly died on you.

- If your cell phone is being used as your primary phone, be certain to sign up for a voice mail service so that you don't miss any messages.

- If you don't use your cell phone too frequently, consider buying prepaid cell phone cards, which are available at convenience stores. On a per-minute basis, they are more expensive than many regular cellular service plans but may be cheaper for you in the long run if you're an infrequent user.

USING A PAGER

Pagers are yet another way of staying in touch. There are two primary systems:

- **A numeric beeper.** This is the oldest and simplest paging system. The numeric system provides the telephone number of the person trying to reach you. However, there is a significant drawback for the job hunter: Because you may receive calls from people whose numbers you won't recognize, it can make returning a telephone call awkward: "Hello, this is Joe Jones. Someone beeped me at this number . . . ?" One way the numeric system can work for you is if you're being beeped by someone who has taken the real message for you—a roommate, a spouse, an accommodating secretary. Then you can call in to that person for a complete message.

- **An alphanumeric system.** With these more expensive units, you can receive short text messages. In addition to receiving a telephone number you learn that Sarah Smith from the ABC Company called.

USING AN ANSWERING MACHINE

We all call homes where the family sings or the toddler records the outgoing message. Even if you've done this in the past, rerecord your message before starting your job hunt. Even when a potential employer knows he's calling you at home, you want to create a businesslike image. Be sure your message is brief and to the point. If you have an answering machine that offers callers access to different voice mailboxes for various members of the family, tell the caller how to circumvent the message if possible, and set up the system so that you're the first and most accessible message box.

If roommates or other family members ever check messages without you, again stress the importance of writing everything down and saving the messages.

One Other Message Option

Well-paid executives who are job hunting may want to enlist the aid of a "virtual assistant." This service, acting like a secretary of sorts, answers the phone, places calls, takes messages, or offers callers a "search" option ("Should I find him or her for you?"). Then based on preprogrammed information you've entered (ranging from a single telephone number to a series of numbers for the places you'll be that day), the service finds you and relays the message that someone has called, permitting you to get right back to the person if necessary.

This "virtual assistant" also keeps track of a calendar and a telephone directory and can look up a number for you, reads e-mail to you over the phone, and you can preprogram it for your special interests so that you have business news, sports scores, or regular news available to you whenever you check in.

"TO DO" ITEM #8:

Decide how people will reach you and arrange to have messages taken.

ARRANGING FOR FAXES

When they say, "Please fax me . . ." you have a few options. Today most people assume that everyone has access to a fax machine. Here's how to make certain you have an authoritative reply when they ask for a fax.

- Consider purchasing a fax machine. Prices have dropped significantly in recent years, and many fax machines are now being sold as telephone/fax machines, fax/answering machines, or printer/scanner/fax machines. If you're in the market for any of these pieces of equipment anyway, investigate whether or not you can have a fax machine included as part of the unit. Even if you get a job within the first month, you'll find that the fax will remain a great convenience.

- If you don't want to invest in a new piece of equipment now, visit one or more "office centers" or "mailing centers" in your area, and ask about faxing services. Any business that offers faxing will accept faxes for you as well. You should have this fax number handy for the time when someone says, "Could you fax me your resumé?"

"TO DO" ITEM #9:
Make arrangements so that you can both send and receive faxes.

KEEP IT SIMPLE

1. **Treat your job search as professionally as you would any job.**

2. **Devise a way for people to get in touch with you (regular phone, cell phone, beeper).**

3. **Work out a system to be certain you receive all messages.**

PART TWO

JOB

SEARCH

PREP

4
DREAMING BIG:
WHAT DO YOU WANT TO DO WITH YOUR LIFE?

WHAT'S AHEAD

Differentiating Between Dreams and Goals
Working Through Your Dreams to Get to Your Goals
Worksheet
Getting Ideas
Identifying Your Next Step

Readers' note: If you already have a specific career goal, then skip directly to Chapter Five. The purpose of Chapter Four is to help those who are still defining what they want to do with their lives.

"I want to be an astronaut."

"I'm going to be an actress."

"I wish I could be a rock star."

"I'm going to be president."

When children express their goals, they speak in terms of their dreams—what each thinks would be the best job in the world. They are unaffected by life's realities which so often interfere with grand plans.

These dreams don't have to die. More and more people are finding ways to build on what they wanted all along. On weekends my family and I sometimes go to hear a successful rock band—it's made up of a group of middle-aged accountants and lawyers who have created part-time jobs for themselves doing something they love.

I'm even more fortunate—I get to do what I love full-time. Since I was a child I've loved organizing and "running my own show." I was a child who always knew where everything was and arrived everywhere on time. My entrepreneurial spirit dates back to those early years, too. I used to write scripts, hire talent (the neighborhood kids), locate a stage to use, design costumes, create a program, get candy, sell tickets, stage manage the show, and divide the profits. I turned what I enjoy most into a business. I couldn't have dreamt of this profession while I was growing up—it didn't even exist then. But this is proof that if you keep working at what you love and do best, you may be amazed at what can develop!

As for the budding astronaut—there's hope for him, too, by letting his dream provide a vision. He may not become someone who flies in spaceships, but if he does his homework he'll realize that there are many space-related jobs that may blend his youthful dream and his adult skills and interests.

That's why goal setting is so important. Dreams are idealized desires; goals have logical steps for getting there. That's why "dreams to goals" is the focus of this chapter.

DIFFERENTIATING BETWEEN DREAMS AND GOALS

Within your earliest childhood dream is the root of something you may really wish to achieve. Part of goal setting involves looking at your dreams and deciding what part you want to hold on to.

The "actress" may not really care about being on Broadway, but she may want to be in front of people—this could lead to a career in television, in teaching, or in corporate training.

The "rock star" may have based this aspiration on a love of music. If he explores different jobs he can be anything from a sound engineer in a music studio to a marketing executive for a music company.

Most adults have moved beyond the actress/astronaut/rock star stage, but the dreams voiced are still only platforms from which true jobs need to be identified. As you can see from the following chart, a lot of questions precede turning a dream into a goal:

If your dream is	Then your goal could range from
I want a job where I get to travel.	Pilot to investment banker
I want to work with children.	Teacher to pediatric surgeon
I want to work outdoors.	Waterfront activities director at a beach resort to landscape architect

WORKING THROUGH YOUR DREAMS TO GET TO YOUR GOALS

Like the people cited above, you may have a general idea of the work you'd like to do. The following worksheet will help to make your goals more specific. Thinking carefully about the questions and answering them may take some people a few days, but don't spend any longer on it. If you don't have answers by that time, it means that more research is necessary, and it's best to get out and start learning more about various professions than to let a few unanswered questions bog you down.

WORKSHEET

With some of the following questions, you may have only one answer. In other cases, you may be torn between several choices. Go ahead and write them all down. You can narrow the field later on, or pursue job leads in several different areas, and then decide which is right for you.

In what field do you hope to work? (medicine, broadcasting, retail, public service, education, etc.) _____

_____

_____

_____

Do you already have (or know of) a specialty you'd like to pursue? (teaching, marketing, writing, graphic arts, scientific research, etc.) _____

_____

_____

_____

Do you already have certain skills you would like to use in your work? Or do you have specific skills you'd like to acquire for a job? (cooking, computer programming, law research, accounting, nursing, etc.) _____

_____

_____

_____

Are there specific values that are important to you for your job? (saving the environment, working with the disabled or underprivileged, furthering medical research, etc.) _____

_____

_____

_____

Name three things about which you feel passionately. (protecting the rights of children, creating homes that are energy efficient, fighting hunger and homelessness, etc.—there are careers where people can devote themselves to these and similar passions.)

1. _____

2. _____

3. _____

In what kind of environment do you want to work? (outdoors or indoors, traveling, here or abroad, in a store, or in an office, in a hospital, etc.)

_____

_____

_____

How do you like to spend your work days? (teaching, building, working with animals, drawing, looking things up in a library, selling, troubleshooting, etc.) _____

_____

_____

_____

What type of people would you like to be with during the work day? (In some jobs, people primarily interact with co-workers [filmmaking, manufacturing, legal research]; in other jobs, people are almost exclusively with customers or clients [psychotherapy, sales, teaching], so consider this as you answer the question. If you prefer to work alone, note that here.) _____

_____

_____

_____

What level of responsibility do you want in your job now? And in the future? (Some people aspire to run the company; others really don't ever want to be in charge. Note down your preference.) _____

_____

_____

_____

Consider hierarchy within various professions. (Do you want to work in a big company/corporate environment with bosses above your bosses? Or do you think you'd prefer working in a smaller organization where most of management reports to the company owner?) _____

_____

_____

_____

What aspirations do you have for lifestyle and/or pay? (These two are intertwined. The more opulent the lifestyle the greater the need for higher pay.) _____

_____

_____

_____

Where would you like your job to be located? (Most people will probably have their eye on a specific community [for some, New York City and Los Angeles are big draws], but if you're at a stage of life when you could move, you can either identify a specific city or town or describe it by community size and/or area of the country.) _____

_____

_____

_____

"TO DO" ITEM #10:

Fill out worksheet. Have it completed by _____.
(Set a date no more than three days from today.)

By working through these questions, you have identified many of the components you want to have in your ideal job. Unfortunately, few people find jobs that have everything, so your next task involves setting priorities. Go back through the list and mark the three things you wrote down that are most important to you.

1. _____

2. _____

3. _____

Good work! As you move on to the next step, you have a way to describe to people what you are looking for.

GETTING IDEAS

Your next job is to identify some of the companies and/or jobs that might be right for you:

- Talk to everyone you meet—from the dental hygienist who cleans your teeth to your brother-in-law—about what they do and what your interests are. You'll learn a lot about a variety of professions. The hygienist's sister may work in a field that sounds perfect for you.

- Visit the library. Ask the reference librarian to point you toward books about various careers. In addition to the government book *The Occupational Outlook Handbook,* there is a wealth of information on jobs categorized by field, by area of the country, by level of pay, and all sorts of other categories. Set aside an hour for your first visit so you can select the books that will be most helpful to you. Then write down on your calendar a date when you can go for another visit and go through the books that focus best on your specific interests.

- The online services and the Internet have many career resources. Spend some time at home or at the library going online and investigating different job sites and reading bulletin boards. It may give you some new ideas.

- Take a battery of career aptitude tests that are administered by career counselors. (Get a referral from a friend.) These tests can help you pinpoint your strengths and weaknesses and may provide you with new ideas for careers to pursue.

"TO DO" ITEM #11:

Research job possibilities by talking to people, looking at job reference material at the library, and visiting sites on the Internet.

IDENTIFYING YOUR NEXT STEP

If you're still somewhat undecided about what career path you want to pursue, don't give up. Write down the two, three, four, or five job possibilities that interest you. As you progress through the book, you'll find it easier and easier to decide what's right for you.

KEEP IT SIMPLE

1. Reexamine your dreams and assess how they can be turned into specific job goals.

2. Consider how you want to spend your days, what type of people with whom you'd like to work, and what level of responsibility you'd like to assume.

3. Investigate types of jobs by doing some research.

5

SETTING
YOUR GOALS

WHAT'S AHEAD

Formulating Your Goals
Writing Them Down
Helpful Hints

Most people spend more time planning their vacations than they spend thinking through the career path they want to pursue. Though you have yet to look at one want ad or go on a single job interview, the time you're spending now is going to make a big difference to you later on. Not only will it assure you that the job you find is right for you, but because of all the introspection you've done, it's likely to shorten the time you spend actually looking for a job.

Some of you may have skipped Chapter Four and come directly to Chapter Five because you already have a job in mind—you just need to find an opening. However, even if you know what type of job you want, it's important to take a few minutes to focus on the quick exercises in this chapter. By examining today's goals as well as those you have for two and ten years from now, it will help you judge what job is right for today as well as the future.

You need to acknowledge your personal vision before you can expect any of it to materialize. Then your goals will become clear, and you'll have a decision-making framework that will help in every aspect of your life.

FORMULATING YOUR GOALS

- Be specific about each goal. If you want to be a speech pathologist, consider whether you want to work with children or with the elderly (such as stroke victims).

- Many goals will require certain steps prior to achieving that goal, and you may need to do some research before knowing what's involved. If you don't know what is required to become a licensed physical therapist, then you will need to investigate the necessary steps to prepare for this profession. Once you learn what they are, they will be tasks to write down on the "Short-Term Goals" section of your goal sheets.

WRITING THEM DOWN

The goals you establish should be written down—it's a good way to promise yourself you'll keep them:

- Take three pieces of paper, or use the work pages provided. On the first, write down what you would like to be doing in ten years (working as a dentist? Running your own design studio? Retraining and getting a job in the computer industry? Having flexible work so that you can schedule around your children?). Take several days to consider what you want your future to hold, and then settle on the one or two long-range career plans upon which you'd like to focus.

- Record on the second sheet what you would like to be doing in two years. Perhaps you'd like to have a management job within two years, or have carved out a spot for yourself in a new field. Or if your long-range goal requires advanced education (such as going to business school or getting a Ph.D.), then on this sheet of paper you should note down what you would need to be doing during the next two years to accomplish these long-range goals.

6 mos, • Short-term goals belong on your third sheet of paper. If you have to apply to graduate schools as part of your long-range plan, then a short-term goal should include investigating schools and taking the entrance exams.

"TO DO" ITEM #12:

Fill out goal sheets by _____.
(This should take no longer than five days.)

IN TEN YEARS I WOULD LIKE TO:

(Write what you see yourself doing and note down the career goals you would like to have achieved.) _____

_____

_____

_____

IN TWO YEARS I WOULD LIKE TO:
(Write what you see yourself doing and note down the career goals you would like to have achieved.) _____

_____

_____

_____

_____

MY SHORT-TERM (SIX-MONTH) GOALS ARE:
(Some of these goals will need to be steps on the way to achieving your longer-term goals.) _____

_____

_____

_____

_____

HELPFUL HINTS

- As you make your plans, don't try to accomplish the impossible. If you work full-time, enrolling in two night courses in a new field may be unrealistic; start with one class so that the goals you set are achievable.

- Put your goal sheets in your Job Search Notebook so that you'll have them for easy reference.

- Goals can and should be reviewed every six months (about the time when you should be setting new short-term goals) and revised as needed. Write this "review session" on your calendar. You may start law school and discover that becoming a corporate attorney isn't for you; however, you'd really like to do public defense work. Examine your goal sheets to determine what other issues this may affect (type of experiential summer job you want, possible volunteer work you could do to learn more about the profession, etc.).

K EEP IT SIMPLE

(1) Setting career goals will provide a decision-making framework that will help in every aspect of your life.

(2) Be very specific in both the goals you set and the steps that are necessary in order to reach them.

(3) Be realistic about what you can achieve in a certain period of time.

6

YOUR SELLING POINTS:

WHAT YOU HAVE TO OFFER

WHAT'S AHEAD

Identifying Your Selling Points

Identifying Specific Skills

Your Personal Assessment

Putting Your Goals and Your Selling Points Side by Side

Create a Descriptive Paragraph About Your Skills

Completing Your "Calling Card"

More Good News

"I don't know exactly how I will fit in at a marketing firm," says a college grad who spent four years working on the college newspaper.

"I don't like practicing law anymore," says a 50-year-old gentleman who has picked up the education credits he needs in order to be hired as a teacher, but was baffled as to what he should say to convince administrators that he should be hired over a 22-year-old.

"I haven't done that much," says a woman who has not worked in five years. She did, however, just run a carnival that brought in a record-breaking amount of money for her children's school.

A fellow who was ready to leave the political arena wondered how applicable his skills are to a public relations firm.

Each of these people have one thing in common: They don't know what they have to offer their future employers. Yet each has a unique background and a set of skills that can help them pursue a career in a new field. What each needs to do is identify the skills he or she has in order to present well to others.

IDENTIFYING YOUR SELLING POINTS

When you select a doctor, an accountant, a builder, or a gardener, there is some reason why you select that professional over another—the person has an expertise you want. You may have heard the doctor "has good rapport with patients," or is an "excellent diagnostician"; the accountant may be known for tackling complex assignments; the builder for doing "on time" work; and the gardener for his or her splendid results. Whatever the reason you've been drawn to them, each had a strength—a "calling card"—that brought you there.

People who land good jobs have taken the time to create a calling card for themselves—they've thought about their past achievements, and know the skills at which they excel.

Take a few minutes to work through these exercises. After finalizing your answers here, write them down on three-ring paper so that you can insert the paper into your Job Search Notebook.

Exercise 1

Write down five things you've accomplished during your life about which you're the most proud:

1. _____

2. _____

3. _____

4. _____

5. _____

Exercise 2

Write down five job-related tasks you've done that you've enjoyed the most (meeting with customers, writing a computer program, studying wildlife habits, etc.). Tasks done for a volunteer organization can be included. If you're a student, consider summer jobs and/or work you've done for school organizations.

1. _____

2. _____

3. _____

4. _____

5. _____

IDENTIFYING SPECIFIC SKILLS

Some of the items listed in Exercises 1 and 2 may be perfect for your resumé: "raised a record-breaking amount of money for _____ organization," "orchestrated a special event that heightened public awareness of _____ ," or "started Little League organization in a community where it never existed before." Each of these are remarkable accomplishments that almost certainly belong on your resume.

In some cases, the accomplishment you wrote down may not be directly applicable to a job, but the skills you used will be. For example, planning and arranging a family trip to China isn't exactly something you'd write on your resumé, but there are many skills involved in it: researching (airlines, hotels, etc.), logistics (when can you go, where can you go in that period of time), scheduling (the itinerary), budgeting (getting the best fares and deals), and so forth. While you may not have enjoyed the logistics and scheduling, you may be very proud of the special deals you got on plane fares and hotel rates, and this skill is something you may want to highlight as you begin your job search.

Exercise 3

Write down five things you're really good at or things you enjoy that don't necessarily have to do with work you've done (good with children, excellent craftsperson, gardening or party planning skills, etc.).

1. _____

2. _____

3. _____

4. _____

5. _____

"TO DO" ITEM #13:

Take time to give Exercises 1, 2, and 3 careful thought.

YOUR PERSONAL ASSESSMENT

Earlier in this chapter you read about how people seek out professionals about whom they've heard good things: "excellent craftsman" or "crackerjack lawyer" are the types of descriptions that might get a carpenter or an attorney some additional work.

Now your task is to decide how you would like to describe yourself. Your list from Exercise 3 (which will be filed in your Job Search Notebook) might read something like this:

1. **I'm good at planning events.**

2. **I'm good at raising money.**

3. **I'm good at getting other people to work well together.**

4. **I'm good at teaching older people new skills.**

5. **I'm good at delegating tasks.**

- If you feel there are other things at which you excel, add them to the list.

- Put an asterisk by the three sentences that make you feel best about yourself.

Exercise 4

- Consider these action words and circle those that are particularly appropriate for you.

- Some of the words may remind you of words people use to describe you—"she's so organized" or "he motivates that committee like no one else ever has." Try to recall things people have always said about you as you go through this list.

achieved	budgeted
analyzed	built
assembled	cared for
awarded	coached

computerized
conceived
conducted
coordinated
created
cultivated
cut
demonstrated
designed
developed
directed
engineered
established
established rapport
expanded
forecast
hired
implemented
increased
increased productivity
initiated
installed
introduced
invented
investigated
launched

led
located
managed
marketed
motivated
moved
organized
oversaw
planned
produced
(achieved) proficiency
raised
realized increase
received
redesigned
reduced
revamped
reviewed
saved
secured (money, usually)
sold
stayed on schedule
supervised
supported
taught
trained

- As you review these terms, you may have other words that come to mind. Add them in.

- Now go back and review the words you circled. On another sheet of paper (three-ring so that this page can be inserted into your Job Search Notebook), complete the sentence for each word you circled: "trained whom?" "organized what?" "cared for whom?" "launched what?"

"TO DO" ITEM #14:
Create a running list of accomplishments.

Putting Your Goals and Your Selling Points Side by Side

An ad agency art director who is hiring a graphic artist wants to hear about creativity, self-discipline, and the ability to work well with business people, among other things. From a hiring standpoint, he or she doesn't care that you work well with children or that you are an expert rock climber. For this reason, your next task is to evaluate your selling points.

Just as an ad has a headline and then more descriptive text later on, what you're trying to capture is what needs to be in *your* headline for particular markets. While all of your accomplishments contribute to your overall strength as an employee, it's important to select the two or three items that are most relevant in order to present them first.

- If you have more than one possible career goal, use a separate piece of paper for each goal, writing a specific goal at the top of each sheet.

- Take a look at your selling points and decide which accomplishments would be helpful in pursuing each of your career goals. (Some accomplishments—being well organized—would be relevant for all career goals.) Perhaps you were a buyer for a major department store, but you've taken five years off to raise your children, during which you wrote and edited a community newsletter.

— If one of your goals concerns running a local store for the owner, then your selling points should emphasize your retail background.

— If you're also considering whether to follow your youthful dream of getting a job that works toward government improvement, then you might emphasize the knowledge you've gained by working on the community newsletter and interacting with all aspects of your local governing body.

Career Goal:

List applicable skills from Exercise 4. Use a separate sheet of paper if you have more than one career goal.

"TO DO" ITEM #15:

Condense your accomplishment list by matching the career goals you've set for yourself with the accomplishments that are relevant to those goals.

CREATE A DESCRIPTIVE PARAGRAPH ABOUT YOURSELF

- Write these sentences up as a very short paragraph that describes what you're best at. As you'll see from the examples, the paragraphs are a blend of strong personal qualities with specific job experience.

  — Conscientious, hardworking computer programmer. Analyst with five-years' experience working with a team that developed state-of-the-art computer equipment for payroll departments. Proficient at trouble-shooting using data analyzer equipment.

  — High-energy, results-oriented store manager for major grocery store chain (five years) with excellent reputation for increasing sales and bringing the store expenses in under budget.

  — Experienced copywriter of direct mail solicitations with track record for increasing direct response for clients by at least 27 percent for each mailing. Reputation for creative ideas and fast delivery time.

COMPLETING YOUR "CALLING CARD"

Now you have a way of introducing your situation—even to those who know you well: "I'm very creative and also well organized. I've supervised a lot of special events for nonprofit organizations, and I'd like to do this for a major corporation."

Once you have identified your selling points—your "calling card"—you have created a way for people to describe you to others. One beautiful Sunday your uncle will be golfing and telling his golf buddy: "Oh, yes, I have a niece who is perfect for your company. She's creative and well organized, and she's run all kinds of dinners for some organizations she's involved in—she's always getting us to come. Can she call someone in your special events department?"

The next thing you know, you'll have the interview you've been wanting!

MORE GOOD NEWS

More good news? Absolutely. Because of the work you've done in this chapter, your resumé is more than half written!

KEEP IT SIMPLE

1. **Identify the important accomplishments in your life.** By doing so, you'll be better prepared to describe what value you bring to any job you want.

2. **Identify specific skills you have that you would enjoy using in your new job.**

3. **Narrow your descriptive sentences about yourself down to a brief paragraph.**

7

RESUMÉ WRITING

WITHOUT PAIN AND SUFFERING

WHAT'S AHEAD

A Special Note About the Purpose of Your Resumé

Styles of Resumés

The Elements of a Resumé

Resumé Worksheet

The Importance of Presentation

Will Your Resumé Survive a Scanning?

Modifying Your Basic Resumé

Don't get writer's block over having to prepare a resumé! You're almost finished:

1. **Because of the work you did in the previous chapter, the more difficult part of your resumé preparation is behind you.** What you have left requires very little time at all.

2. **You needn't sweat about resumés the way so many people do—a neat resumé with no misspellings is really what's required.** This piece of paper is going to get a couple of minutes of attention. It needs to present you well, but it doesn't need months and months of work poured into it.

3. **You also needn't consider this resumé "final."** It's truly a resumé-in-progress. What you're going to create now is a basic resumé that will be adapted to the various situations you encounter. If you learn that the person who is interviewing you was a member of the same fraternity you were in, suddenly your fraternity affiliation from college becomes an important element to add to your resumé. Winning resumés have generally been slanted for a particular opening—that's what I'll teach you to do here.

A SPECIAL NOTE ABOUT THE PURPOSE OF YOUR RESUMÉ

When an interviewer meets any job candidate, he not only considers how the person presents him- or herself and what's on the resumé, but there's another primary concern on the interviewer's mind:

"Is this the person who can solve my problems?"

Whether the person is hiring a forward-thinking principal, an ace mechanic, a brilliant defense attorney, or a secretary who can get things done, the interviewer wants to know *how you can solve his/her problems.*

In your interview you will do what you can to persuade him/her of your ability to help, but in the meantime, your resumé must reflect how you have solved problems for others. As you prepare your resumé, keep the focus on your accomplishments—how you improved sales, made functional tasks go more smooothly, or created an innovative public relations campaign for your previous employers.

STYLES OF RESUMÉS

There are three primary styles of resumés:

The Chronological Resumé

With this style of resumé, your experience is presented in chronological order; the classic form of this resumé is primarily a list of your jobs and where you attended school. It is appropriate when applying for a job within the same industry (or the same company) where those who are interviewing candidates are well aware of the responsibilities and scope of previous jobs.

The Functional Resumé (also known as the skills resumé)

With a functional resumé, experience is clustered under major skill areas. If you're strong in mathematical ability and want to communicate this strength, you would cluster all the types of accounting or mathematical experience you'd had under a single heading. The "skills" style is the resumé of choice when you're trying to show how your abilities fit well into a specific job objective. It's also a good format to choose if you are a student without much paid work experience or if you've had some time out of the workforce. While jobs are usually catalogued at the bottom of the resumé, there is less emphasis on positions and dates than with a chronological resumé.

The Combination Resumé

A resumé that is a combination of the two styles of resumés is also quite practical and popular. Job experience is presented chronologically, but each position mentioned is followed by results-oriented descriptions of skills. When in doubt, this style of resumé should be used. It not only lists your employment but describes it as well.

THE ELEMENTS OF A RESUMÉ

Here are the typical elements one generally sees on a resumé. Some are necessary for every resumé; some will only be used under certain circumstances:

- Identification (name, contact information)
- Introductory paragraph
- Related and/or previous experience
- Professional memberships
- Volunteer work
- Honors and achievements
- Education
- Personal information
- References

Here's what you need to know about each:

Identification (your name, address, and phone number)

- Use your full name for a more professional presentation; as an employer gets to know you, you can tell him or her about your nickname.

- Highlight your phone number by skipping a space before it, or placing it on the side (see the examples at the end of the chapter). Someone who wants to hire you is more likely to phone than write. (As discussed in Chapter 3, it's important that you've made arrangements so that you can be contacted by phone or pager at all times.)

- If you don't have a permanent address, rent a post office box or make an arrangement with one of the mail centers in your town (or the town in which you're job hunting).

- If you've got an e-mail address, add it to your contact information.

Introductory Paragraph

Just like a well-written ad, you need to extract what is important in your resumé (this is an organized way to approach employers because it saves them time). Salient information belongs in an opening paragraph, which generally takes the form of a "job objective" or a "qualifications summary" paragraph. The type of paragraph you choose primarily depends on how much you know about the job for which you're applying:

The Job Objective Paragraph: Citing a specific job objective ("desires management job overseeing human resources department") has its place, but writing down your goal on paper can limit you (what if there are no openings for human resource managers?), so you want to use this type of paragraph wisely. A job objective is best used under two circumstances:

1. **You are sending your resumé after having spoken to someone at the company about a specific opening.** Under these circumstances, the job objective you write will, of course, be specifically tailored to the opening that has been described to you—making your objective and their opening an exact fit.

2. **Your past work experience does not match the work you are seeking; however, you have other credentials that make you well-suited for a new type of employment.** For example, a person who has worked in banking for ten years but has achieved licensing credentials for physical therapy must state clearly on her resumé what her current goal is: "Fully licensed physical therapist seeks job working

in sports medicine." Otherwise, any interviewer hiring physical therapists would be quite curious as to why he had received a resumé from a former banker.

Qualifications Summary: Remember the two- or three-sentence description of yourself that you created in Chapter 6? This description will work as your "qualifications summary." Evaluate it to be sure that it's a good combination of past experience and current qualifications: "Eight years management experience overseeing insurance agency which doubled in size during that period; qualified to oversee departments as diverse as personnel, accounting, and technical services."

As you can see, these paragraphs can be very helpful to people doing hiring because they give a quick picture of who you are and why you're qualified.

Related and/or Previous Experience:

- If your career path is following a predictable pattern for your industry, then this category on your resumé will be "Previous Experience."

- If you are changing careers, then split this section in two parts: "Related Experience" should be first, and it should include any and all tasks—even volunteer—that give you insight into or knowledge of the field in which you're job hunting. List your other work experience under "Previous Experience." Though the fact that you worked as a salesperson for four years while going to college may not be relevant for getting a job as a dentist, it does tell an employer that you are resourceful, reliable, and willing to work hard.

- This section (or sections) lists the job title, the employer, and the dates.

- On a functional or a combination resumé, also include short descriptions of the work you did and/or specific accomplishments. Simply listing "office administrator" or "art director" doesn't tell anyone what your responsibilities or accomplishments were in the job.

- Refer to Chapter 6 for a list of your various accomplishments. Slot those descriptions of accomplishments under the job titles you're listing. As an art director, some of the responsibilities you include might be:

  — oversaw the work of 30 artists and designers;

  — headed creative team responsible for new seasonal lines two times per year;

  — ran quality control when wallpaper went into production twice each year

- If you've been in the workforce for 15–20 years, be certain that you are using up-to-date terminology in describing your responsibilities. Often the work is the same, but the task itself is now described differently. Don't date yourself by using "old-fashioned" language.

- If the work you are listing is volunteer, make your presentation of it as professional as possible, while still indicating that you did it as a volunteer. (If volunteer work is directly relevant to the job for which you're applying, then it is appropriate to list it under the "work experience" section, so long as it's noted that you did it for no pay. Keep reading for suggestions on how to handle other types of volunteer work.) The person applying to be hired as a stage manager for a dinner theater company might write: "Stage managed eight straight plays and three musicals during a three-year period while working as a volunteer at Mar-Bel Community Theater."

- When citing dates of employment, note the years, not the months.

- If you have not had much work experience to describe on your resumé, look around to see if there is any part-time or volunteer work you could do while job hunting that would bolster credentials in the field in which you'd like to work.

Professional Memberships

- This category is optional. If you are active in organizations that relate to the field where you want to work, then citing your involvement is a plus.

- If you are listing an organization and you're an officer, say so.

Volunteer Work

- Volunteer work should be included under three circumstances (and then only if there is space on the page). In the first circumstance cited below, the work can be listed in the "work experience" section of your resumé; in the two other situations, the work should be listed under a "volunteer work" heading.

1. **When the volunteer work is directly applicable to the next job you're seeking (as described previously).**

2. **If you have very deep involvement in an organization and are so active in it that it's a vital part of your existence, then you may feel a need to include it.** And indeed, if you've spearheaded the creation of a soup kitchen in your community, then employers would be impressed with your initiative, vision, and drive—all of which are excellent qualities for most jobs.

3. **If it makes for interesting conversation.** Perhaps you participate in a local environmental program that is involved in counting a certain species of bird. An interviewer might find that interesting, and a short informal conversation about it may make you more memorable to the interviewer.

Honors and Achievements

- Unless you're just out of college, these should be restricted to honors and achievements that have occurred since graduation. If you were honored by the chamber of commerce as Citizen of the Year or if you were the all-time top salesperson for your company, these achievements should be highlighted.

Education

- Cite the schools from which you've graduated (college and post-college training or graduate work, not high school); give the degree received, and the year in which you graduated. (If you're in your thirties or older, you can almost certainly drop the year—anyone who cares how old you are will be able to make a rough guess based on your resumé.)

- If you are a recent graduate, place this information near the top of the page, right after your identification. Those with more work experience should place it as one of the final resumé categories. Once you've been out working for a few years, your work experience becomes more relevant than your educational experience.

- Recent graduates also need to include their grade point averages. For jobs in finance and computer science, including your GPA is imperative. If you've been in good standing or your grades are at the top of the range, then this will tell the employer that you're a hard worker; if they haven't been top-flight, there are ways to still present yourself in a good light. For example, if your GPA in your major is higher than your overall grade point average, then list it beside the overall GPA, showing employers that you're doing well in your chosen field. Or if your grades have improved progressively throughout your college years, calculate your junior and senior years separately and list them. Employers will be respectful of effort and the resulting accomplishment. For young applicants, leaving your GPA off the resumé entirely will only raise suspicion.

Personal Information

- This section is being included less and less. The days of providing height, weight, and marital status are over.

- Unless your experience is so unique that you know exactly what **must** go into this section, then skip it altogether.

References

- Don't waste space on your resumé listing your references or how to contact them.

- You also needn't waste a line writing "References available upon request." Any employer knows that he can ask a job candidate for references, and he will—if he wants or needs them.

RESUMÉ WORKSHEET

It should take you only 30 minutes or less to fill out the following worksheet. Once you've done so, all you have left to do is to place it in an appropriate format:

Name _____

Address _____

_____

E-mail address _____

Phone _____

Pager (if appropriate) _____

Work Experience: For each job you've held, create the following listing:

1. Job title, place of employment, dates.

2. Any special skills needed or acquired while on the job.

3. Accomplishments: refer back to Chapter 6 where you listed special accomplishments. If no accomplishments from a particular job were on this list, feel free to add in achievements obtained in this position.

1. Job title, place of employment, dates:

_____

_____

2. Skills used or acquired:

_____

_____

3. Accomplishments:

_____

_____

1. Job title, place of employment, dates:

_____

_____

2. Skills used or acquired:

_____

_____

3. Accomplishments:

_____

_____

1. Job title, place of employment, dates:

_____

2. Skills used or acquired:

_____

3. Accomplishments:

_____

_____

1. Job title, place of employment, dates:

_____

2. Skills used or acquired:

_____

3. Accomplishments:

_____

_____

1. Job title, place of employment, dates:

_____

_____

2. Skills used or acquired:

_____

_____

3. Accomplishments:

_____

_____

Professional organizations in which you're active:

_____

_____

Any volunteer work you feel you'd like to list:

_____

_____

Honors and achievements:

_____

_____

Education (and any special job preparation training such as job certification, etc.): List the highest level or most recent first (institution, town and state, degree). Recent grads should also note GPAs:

_____

_____

_____

_____

Relevant courses, awards, experiences:

_____

_____

Military experience _____

Any special training received _____

Military awards or honors _____

"TO DO" ITEM #17:

Fill out resumé worksheet.

THE IMPORTANCE OF PRESENTATION

The presentation of your resumé is almost as important as what the document says about you. Clarity and a good clean look are vital in presenting the best of your background quickly. Here's how:

- Prepare your resumé on a computer. It makes it easy to adapt for different job interviews, and you can update it easily. If you don't have a good quality printer, put your resumé on a disk and find someone who will let you use his or her printer.

- If you need an outside service to do this for you, make certain they give you a disk with your resumé on it. Then family members or friends can help you with updates.

- Keep it short. Resumés are generally one page; two pages only if absolutely necessary (long list of appropriate jobs to describe or heavy academic credentials).

- Take a brief glance at your resume, and assess how it looks. Is it well laid out? Pleasing to the eye? Does it make good use of white space so that your eye is drawn to the most important parts of the resume? Does it look professional?

- Now read it closely for content. Does it make sense for the job you want?

- Proofread your resume carefully for typographical, grammatical, and punctuation errors. A resume with mistakes offers an employer a good reason for moving on to the next candidate.

- Your resumé should be reviewed by a friend or family member who not only knows you but also understands the business world well enough to give you constructive feedback. (If you know someone in the field who would help you, that's even better.) Select one person whom you respect to go over it with you, and then don't keep soliciting opinions from others. When it comes to someone else's resumé, everyone's an expert, and you could waste a lot of time with editing and reediting it.

- As recommended in Chapter 2, use a good quality paper for printing out copies of your resume. Regular copy paper will not make the best presentation. Look at samples at a stationery store—ivory or white is best.

So now that you have your resumé, what are you going to do with it? Many job hunters think that the way to find a job is printing a hundred resumés and mailing them out to a hundred personnel offices. That's one of the least effective ways of looking for a job!

The best use of a resumé is a very targeted one:

— Your aunt knows someone who is hiring early education instructors;

— A headhunter obtained your name from a friend of yours, and she has called and described a specific management position to you;

— You're applying for a job you read about on a company's Web site;

— You met an upper management fellow from a major corporation at a meeting of your professional organization, and he said, "Send me your resumé! I think I have a job for you."

In each of these situations, you have learned something about a possible opening, so you have some familiarity with the requirements of the job. This lets you tailor your resumé to better fit the company to which you're sending it.

In several of the above examples, something positive is at work for you: a contact has been made by you or on your behalf, meaning that a person will be expecting to receive your resumé. Sending out one single anticipated resumé is worth more than sending out a full hundred unanticipated ones.

WILL YOUR RESUMÉ SURVIVE A SCANNING?

If you've read about how some employers are using software to scan the mountains of resumés they receive to weed out those who don't use certain key words on their resumés, don't worry. Sending a resumé to a place so impersonal that it's going to be read by a scanner isn't the path to getting a job—the type of job search you're going to launch is a person-to-person approach, not a person-(you)-to-scanner one. However, rest assured that if your resumé does get put through a scanner, your resumé will be pulled out for any and all relevant jobs. Scanners are looking for certain types of qualifications based on terminology, and if you've put together a new resumé and have been careful about using up-to-date terminology, you'll be fine.

MODIFYING YOUR BASIC RESUMÉ

At this point you may be so relieved to have finished your basic resumé that you may have groaned at the very thought of ever changing a single word. In many ways you're right—you're to be congratulated on finishing this resumé, and you ought to be able to give it a rest.

However, as you start going out on your first interviews, you'll begin to analyze whether you and a potential job are a good fit. In many cases you won't be: they want someone who doesn't mind traveling three weeks per month; you really love being home as many evenings as you can. When *your* goals and *their* opening match, you're going to want to be the first applicant in the door who says, "I'm perfect for the job, and here's why!" If you've documented your "match" in your resumé, it will be easier for the person doing the interviewing to sell you to the rest of the department. (Remember, most interviewers have to justify a "new hire" to other people within the company, so that's why it's vital that you give them lots of ammunition for why you're so perfect for the job.)

So how do you modify your resumé? By asking yourself the following question before each job interview:

What requirements does this job have that I've already mastered?

Let's suppose you've had experience in front office management jobs in several Boston hotels, and you'd like to be hired as a travel agent for a corporate travel department. Instead of describing how successfully you managed the front office staffs, your job descriptions should now highlight problem solving and knowledge of the travel industry. When you describe what you did in each position you held, stress those qualities.

Or if writing is what you primarily want to do in your next position, and if you're applying for a public relations job, you'll want to emphasize any experience you've had at press release writing and getting publicity. However, if you're interviewing to write and edit a newsletter, then writing and editing are the skills to emphasize. Each time you send out your resumé for a position for which you have applicable experience, show that you already have the background and skills that are needed for the position.

KEEP IT SIMPLE

1. Your resumé will receive just a few minutes of attention, but it's an important few minutes where you need to convey what value you can bring to your future employer.

2. Clarity and error-free presentation are very important in putting together a good resumé.

3. Your resumé should not be used to blanket personnel offices in your search for a job; each resumé should be sent to a particular individual with a specific goal in mind.

Sample functional/chronological resumé

SANDRA FERGUSON
937 Walnut St., Chicago, IL 60637

Phone (312) 555-2233   Fax (312) 555-1122

Qualifications:

Senior executive with over 15 years experience in retail manufacturing, product development, and marketing; ability to prepare and maintain budgets, motivate, and supervise staff, and spearhead strong marketing campaigns.

Professional Experience:

Vice President and Division Manager, Stratford Shoe Company, Chicago, 1997–present

- Report to president of this $200 million manufacturing and marketing company.
- Responsible for direct marketing/merchandising for 12 operating companies, 130 store departments, and 1,430 employees.
- Have developed and been in charge of marketing strategy that has increased sales 40 percent in 3 years.
- Created customer relations program that reduced complaints by 65 percent.

Vice President, Retail Division, Williamton Handbag and Shoe Company, Willamette, Delaware,1990–97

- Reported to senior VP of this $400 million manufacturer, wholesaler, and retailer of women's handbags and shoes.
- Closed less profitable stores realizing a savings of $4 million.
- Developed successful marketing strategy that increased sales by 5 percent.

Director of Manufacturing, Marvin Leather Goods, Lebanon, Pennsylvania, 1988–90

- Reported to VP of Operations of this $150 million manufacturer.

- Helped plan and implement changeover to new equipment, resulting in an increase of 50 percent greater plant efficiency.
- Managed 400 employees and created a flex-time schedule to improve job satisfaction and increase productivity.

Project Engineer, Lilly Leather Company, Lebanon, Pennsylvania, 1986–88

Education:

M.S. Delaware State University, 1985, Major: mechanical engineering
B.S. Lehigh University, 1983

Functional/chronological resumé with job objective

MAX TREADWILL
31819 Wilshire Blvd.
Los Angeles, CA 90024

Phone (213) 555-8899
E-mail: <u>max413;@(host).com</u>

Job Objective:

After 12 years of teaching in elementary schools, I returned to school to obtain the Ph.D. needed to become a school psychologist. After working so closely with children in the classroom, I not only feel qualified to counsel these children, but I have a better understanding of how to coordinate help with a classroom teacher, the single most important person whom a child sees during the school day.

Previous Experience:
Fifth grade teacher, Aberdeen Elementary School, Muncie, IN, 1989–96
- Assisted with transition of students into a 5–8 middle school environment;
- Led first group of team teachers in the new middle school;
- Fifth grade reading and math scores on state tests increased by 5 percent and 3 percent respectively during a four-year period.
- Helped class cope with the deaths of two parents of children in the class; established special grief groups at the time of each death; worked with family members to help ease the pain of the children.

Second grade teacher, Garrison Elementary School, Indianapolis, IN, 1984–89
- Worked cooperatively with other second grade teachers to create shared learning experiences for children;
- Initiated a special program for nonreading second graders so that they lost as little time as possible in acquiring this badly needed skill.

Volunteer Work:
Hospital pediatric ward volunteer; Lakeland General, Muncie, IN, 1994–99
  Worked six-hour shift every other weekend, visiting children on the pediatric ward, talking to them about their illness; playing with them, offering activities.

Education:

Ball State University, Ph.D. program, cum laude, 1999

Ball State University, M.A. in education, 1997

Indiana State University, B.A., 1983

Recent grad resumé

STEPHANIE GALLAGHER

33 Oak Lane

Rye Brook, NY 11565

(914) 555-1122, phone; (914) 555-2233, fax;

e-mail: gallagher;@(host).com

Job Objective:

I would like to work as an admissions counselor for a women's college. Single-sex education still plays an important role in American education, and I would like to participate in helping to attract and select qualified applicants.

Education:

Mar-Fan Women's College, Farmingdale, Massachusetts, B.A., 1999

Grade point average: 3.7

Related Experience:

Receptionist, part-time, Mar-Fan Women's College Admissions Office, 1997–99

- Answered phones and greeted visitors while also helping with the sorting and initial reading of incoming applications;
- Created an organized method for receiving, copying, and sorting applications while getting the appropriate data entered into the computer.

Gold Key Guide, Mar-Fan College, 1996–99

- Gold Key Guide are honors students who are selected to give occasional tours of the campus to visiting families.

Other Experience:

Waitress, Cape Cod, summer of 1998

Counselor for middle school girls, Camp Run-a-Tee, summers 1994–97

Honors and Awards:

Bronze Star award for Gold Key work (given to guide who exemplifies the best spirit, attitude, and ability), 1999

Mar-Fan Honor Society Member, 1997–99

JOHN WILLIAMS
2915 Eighth Avenue
Pueblo, Colorado 81003

(303) 555-4321, phone; (303) 444-1234, fax
e-mail: jwilliams432;@(host).com

Qualifications Summary:

Senior financial executive with 11 years experience with $40 million manufacturing company of excavating equipment. Heavily experienced in all aspects of domestic financial planning. Highly skilled at negotiating favorable rates and terms on major capital requirements.

Major Accomplishments:

Capital Acquisition:

- Developed three-year funding strategy to finance $10 million capital expansion program. Capital acquired on average of 2.45 percent below market rate.
- Was able to maintain financial rating for company despite substantial increase in long-term debt.

Financial Planning:

Oversee leadership development of planning strategy for annual capital requirements.

- Developed and implemented computer system for company so that all

---

accounting systems of all offices at other locations are linked; saved company $1 million by reducing staffing needs for accountants at other locations.

Investor Relations:
- Excellent rapport with industry analysts.
- Maintain wide network of financial contacts in a wide range of financial institutions in the tri-state region where our plants are located.

Employment History:

Quigley Corporation, corporate offices, 1989-present
    Vice president and treasurer (1997-present)
    Director of Corporate Finance (1992-97)
    Senior analyst, Corporate Finance (1990-92)
    Analyst, Corporate Finance (1989-1990)

Education:

    MBA, Harvard Business School, 1989
    Major: Finance

    BA, Colorado State University, 1986
    Major: Financial management, magna cum laude

8

ALL ABOUT COVER LETTERS

WHAT'S AHEAD

The Most Important Words in Your Cover Letter

Preparing an Appealing Cover Letter

Presentation

Your resumé without a cover letter is much like a highway exit without a sign notifying drivers of what exit is approaching. A potential employer is caught off-guard if there's nothing that warns him what's coming and tells him why this particular resumé is of interest.

THE MOST IMPORTANT WORDS IN YOUR COVER LETTER

An employer has a job opening, not because she wants to add to her staff and increase her payroll. She has a job opening because she has a problem to solve—someone is leaving the company or moving within the company or business is booming, and she needs additional help. The most comforting message any employer can receive from a potential employee is this:

I understand your problems, and I'm here to help.

Your cover letter is guaranteed to get attention if you can highlight your applicable skills and how they suit what the employer needs.

Your resumé does a good job of saying who you are; the main goal of your cover letter is placing you (and your resumé) in context with this company, this opening, and this interviewer. You have to say right up front what skills and abilities you have and how you can put them to profitable use.

PREPARING AN APPEALING COVER LETTER

- Get the name of a specific person to whom a letter should be sent—no "Dear Sir" or "Dear Madam" letters.

- Find a way to make a personal connection: you were referred to him by a good friend of hers; you've just met with her boss who said you should contact her; you are best friends with her cousin ("Sarah Smith suggested I contact you . . . "). There's got to be a strong enough connection that the person would have difficulty *not* responding to you. (In Chapter 9 you'll read about how to make these contacts.)

- Be sure you have the correct spelling of the name of the person to whom you're writing. If you've misspelled that, your letter and resumé will go directly into the wastebasket. If you don't have the person's business card, call the company and ask a secretary to slowly spell the name for you.

- Have an agenda for writing. Each cover letter you write will almost certainly have a different goal, ranging from contacting your roommate's father for information about the field of entertainment law, to writing to someone you met at a conference who told you about an opening she had in her software company. In each case, consider exactly what you want to have result from having written the letter:

— You want to spend a short time with the person to get advice about entering the field. Don't ask for an interview. Unless this person is actually doing interviewing for a position, this puts your contact on the defensive (the person won't want to disappoint you) and gives him an immediate reason not to see you: "I don't have a job opening." Instead, ask for "a few minutes" of his or her time, so that you can ask a few questions about the company, or the industry, or some insights into the type of work you're considering. People are flattered at the thought that they are experts, and are likely to try to make time to see you.

— You want to be considered for a specific opening he has in his department in a situation where you have been told of an opening.

— You want her to provide you with names of people whom you can contact about a job.

- <u>Clearly state why you're writing</u>: "I'm going to be in town, and I'm visiting area medical centers to investigate the employment picture." Or: "I'm exploring a possible career change from newspaper work to broadcasting, and I'd love to stop by and see how a local television station is run."

- If your cover letter concerns a specific job opening, **do** <u>express to the person why your qualifications are perfect for the company.</u> Some employers are impressed by a side-by-side comparison chart within your letter. You'll need specific information about the requirements for the job, and then the presentation of employer needs and your qualifications might look like this:

XYZ Company Is Seeking:	My Qualifications:
1 year heavy equipment sales experience	2 years selling heavy equipment for J. Don Equipment Sales
3 years experience with engineering department using heavy equipment	4 years in training department, teaching engineers to use heavy equipment

- **Do** expect to follow up. Even with a dynamite cover letter and resumé, it is rare for the recipient to pick up the phone to call you for an appointment. If all goes well, however, the person will be expecting your call, and when the secretary says: "Joe Smith wants an appointment next week," your contact will say, "Go ahead and set it up!"

PRESENTATION

Just like your resumé, the presentation of your cover letter is very important. The letter must be well-written with no spelling or grammar errors, and the overall look of the letter should be professional.

- Prepare the letter on your computer. While you'll have to tailor your letters to each individual company, there will be elements that will remain the same. This will save time and reduce errors.

- Proofread your letter for both content and grammar or spelling errors. Computer spell-check programs aren't perfect, and they certainly don't spell-check names.

- If you have letterhead stationery, your cover letter should be printed on it. If you've created a letterhead on your computer, then print your letter on the same good quality paper you used for your resumé.

"TO DO" ITEM #18:

Prepare a basic cover letter—one you can adapt each time you need to mail out your resumé.

Sample Cover Letter

Date

Contact Name
Company Name
Full Address

Dear [contact's name]:

Your housemate in graduate school, Mary Smith, is now my professor in my land use law course. She is encouraging me to go into the field of environmental law, with a special emphasis on zoning regulations.

Professor Smith says you have been instrumental in helping countless towns and cities across the nation rewrite their zoning ordinances, and that I should be sure to talk to you before making any career decisions.

I am #2 in my graduating class and have worked on the Law Review for the past two years. I have also had summer jobs relating to this field—one was involved in developing appropriate signage laws for the highway areas around Middletown, Connecticut. Another summer I worked on how to help commercial and residential areas coexist in a densely settled part of Long Island, New York.

I would be very appreciative of a few minutes of your time when I'm in town the first week of May. I'll phone your office next week to see if it would be possible to set up an appointment.

Sincerely,

[Your Name]

KEEP IT SIMPLE

1. **No resumé should be sent out without a cover letter.** The cover letter is necessary to provide perspective as to why your background is appropriate for a company's needs or to provide a reason why a contact should meet with you for an informational session.

2. **Have a specific reason for writing to the contact and state that reason clearly in the letter.**

3. **Expect to follow up.**

PART THREE

STEPPING

OUT

9

WHO IS GOING TO HELP YOU?

BUILDING YOUR SQUAD

WHAT'S AHEAD

Identifying the Team

The Value of Mentors

Where Do Personnel Agencies and Search Firms Fit In?

What About Want Ads and the Internet?

Expanding the Squad

Networking Basics

mbarking on a new undertaking may stir up feelings of that primary emotion, "being all alone." But when it comes to organizing your job search, you not only aren't alone, you can't afford to be alone—it's absolutely vital that you anoint everyone you know as a member of your "Job Search Squad." Not only are **you** going to be looking for a job, but your Uncle Willy, your Aunt Sarah, the fellow you met through your friend, and a professional contact you located through your alumni association are all going to be helping you.

Here's how:

IDENTIFYING THE TEAM

In the "People" section of your notebook, start a running list of anyone and everyone you know who might have advice for you.

- List family members, friends, business associates, and acquaintances. "Willing to help" is the only quality any of these people need. As you'll learn in the next chapter, these people don't have to have a job for you—or even work in the same industry—you're only going to ask them for names of people whom they know who might help you.

- Establish a listing for each person, complete with name, address, telephone and fax number, and e-mail address.

- Note down associations and organizations that might have information that would be of value:

- Your college career office. Almost all colleges continue to help graduates regardless of how long they've been out of school.

- The alumni network. Many institutions have assembled data bases of their alumni specifically to create networking opportunities among all ages of graduates. By contacting the college and getting involved with the network, you should be able to receive a printout of people in the appropriate field.

- Trade associations or professional organizations in your field of interest. The organization itself may have information that will be helpful to you in your search.

- Contacts you meet through networking (see below for suggestions).

- Names of newsmakers in your field who have been written up in the trade or general press recently

THE VALUE OF MENTORS

Welcome to the new age of mentoring. Today instead of waiting for a gray-haired senior executive to take notice of them, workers at all levels of employment are taking matters into their own hands and finding and establishing their own relationships. Some bonds are within the same company and are the traditional older-worker, younger-worker

---

relationship; others are unions that run the gamut from a single peer to a mixed-age group. If you define a mentor as someone who may have a little more experience than you do, cares about helping move your career along, and will offer you guidance then consider these types of mentoring situations:

— a peer who works in your industry and is willing to advise you;

— a friend who works in another industry who is willing to serve as an advisor and cheerleader as you go through this process;

— a support group where everyone agrees to work to support the others;

— a traditional relationship between a senior employee and yourself;

— an online pal who lives miles and miles from you who is willing to send you supportive and knowledgeable e-mail encouragement about the process;

— a family member (this is where unconditional love kicks in) who is willing to keep you going.

The best mentors are those whom you also consider to be good role models, but a perfectly fine mentor is anyone from whom you can learn something—that broadens the possibilities immensely!

While you may feel awkward making an official request for a mentoring "relationship," you'll find that there's no need to ask anyone "to sign on the dotted line" because most people are happy to participate in networking and mentoring. So long as your co-worker or former boss is willing to chat with you, ask about your progress, and make suggestions on your search, consider yourself "mentored."

"TO DO" ITEM #19:

Identify people who can serve as your formal or informal mentor(s). (No need to restrict yourself to one if there are additional possibilities!)

WHERE DO PERSONNEL AGENCIES AND SEARCH FIRMS FIT IN?

While the thought of arriving at a placement office or search firm at 9:00 A.M., explaining the job you want, and letting them get it for you is very appealing, that's not how most jobs are found. The vast majority of people get their jobs through making contacts, setting up interviews, and following up. That's not to say that jobs are *never* obtained through this process. Search firms make high-salary upper management placements, and personnel firms keep support jobs filled. However, maintaining control and expecting to find your job yourself is more likely to bring you the results you want at the time you want them.

Add to your contact list any of the establishments that meet the following criteria:

- Executive search firms do much of their recruiting by networking. If you've been working in a management position, you may have heard from a firm that was looking for names of particular types of candidates. If you liked the person who called you, add him/her to your list. (Remember that executive search firms earn their money from the company that has the opening, and they are at their best when seeking people who have qualifications to move up within the same field. Search firms have less to offer to career changers; anyone changing jobs is a tougher "sell" to the firm's client since that person is unlikely to have the exact credentials required.)

- Personnel agencies mainly place people in temporary positions. However, there are phases in almost everyone's career when this can be of value. Temporary work is no longer just secretarial; all types of positions ranging from attorneys through clerical work are being filled by "temps," and for some, the work develops into a full-time position. Some temporary employees also find that working under these circumstances is a terrific way to check out a company, make contacts, and find out what the firm's employment needs are. If you find yourself applying for a full-time position at a company where you've temped, chances are you'll be high on the list, since the employer already knows you.

WHAT ABOUT WANT ADS AND THE INTERNET?

Jobs can sometimes be found through contacts made through help wanted ads or postings on the Internet. Professions such as teaching do rely on ads to bring them a wide variety of applicants from which they winnow the candidates down to a few. And because the Internet and related services are growing so quickly, a good number of computer programmers, Web designers, and other workers with technical expertise are finding jobs through Internet postings. However, ideally you want to find the person who is hiring for a job **before** the company decides to run an ad or put up a posting—the numbers of letters and resumés received can be truly daunting!

If you're answering ads or Internet postings as part of your job search strategy, answer every one that you find the least bit intriguing. The fact that an employer must wade through so many resumés means that numerically the odds are not as good as when you've been able to make some sort of personal contact.

EXPANDING THE SQUAD

It's important to spend your time during the next few months out in the world so that you can make as many contacts as you can. Think big, think flexible, and think creative to expand your networking possibilities.

The logical places to network are at industry functions and professional meetings that pertain to your field, yet there are many other ways to make valuable contacts. One of the best is to take a course or attend a workshop that has to do with the field in which you want to work. The instructor should definitely go on your "contacts" list, and you'll also be able to develop a nice relationship with the other people in your class.

Another way people make strong contacts is by volunteering for tasks for industry groups. The best "chores" are those with high visibility ("reception committee?") and low burdensome responsibility. Keep in mind that your priority right now should be to take on tasks where you are able to circulate among employed people in the industry.

But networking can take place elsewhere, too—at a part-time retail sales job, doing volunteer work at a local school, when you send out holiday cards (add a note to the cards you send to friends saying what you're up to and then follow up by phone after the beginning of the year), or when you're having dinner or on the tennis court with friends. Everyone you meet is important, so be willing to keep telling people who you are and what it is you're looking for.

As you build your team, remember: networking is a two-way street. In addition to consulting contacts about what you're interested in, ask about each person you meet as well. If you're at a loss as to what to say, ask: "Is there anything I can do for you?" Smart networkers have something to offer in return.

NETWORKING BASICS

- When you attend an event or sign up for a course, set a goal for yourself. Are you looking for general career advice? Contacts in your chosen industry? Contacts at a specific company?

- Before leaving home, work on a 10–15 second introduction of yourself. Don't stop with your last job title—"I'm Mary Miller, and I'm a designer at XXX Company." Describe what you're looking for: "I'm Mary Miller. I'm a sportswear designer for XXX Company, and I'm interested in switching to retailing and would like to become a buyer for a major department store."

- Every time you go anywhere, work at being a good conversationalist. Observe others who seem proficient at the skill. You'll note that they ask lots of questions of others while still knowing how and when to reveal short bits of information about themselves.

- The value of attending a function in order to network is heightened if you practice the art of moving from group to group—something that's difficult to do:

  — Introduce yourself whenever you find yourself next to someone new.

  — After you feel a conversation has been as productive as it's going to be, move on. Nodding or shaking hands and saying, "It was very nice talking to you," or indicating you've got to go check on something or someone will help provide a smooth departure.

- Ask for business cards of those whom you meet, and give out yours when it's appropriate. By giving a person the card, it will make your name more familiar when you call.

- **Always** follow up, and tell contacts that you will. Don't give up control of the situation—what's extremely important to you right now isn't nearly as important to your newly made contact. Even with the best of intentions, people forget. Offer to fax your resumé, or call as a reminder to assure that the next step gets taken. (For the same reason, it's preferable if your contact lets you call his friend using your contact's name as a reference; that way there's no chance for the offer to slip by through neglect.)

- When you arrive home, get out your Job Search Notebook and start adding to the "contacts" section. Make notes about meeting the person and add any tidbits about what the person said that might be helpful to remember later on. Plan to follow up on every lead gained through networking.

- Today networking can also occur on the Internet. While it's not as personal as meeting people face-to-face, if you have an e-mail correspondence with someone who is helping your search along, by all means keep it going!

KEEP IT SIMPLE

1. **Start a running list of anyone and everyone whom you think could be helpful in offering you contacts and/or advice.**

2. **Expand your contacts through networking.** Attend functions, take seminars, volunteer. Talk to everyone whom you meet and tell each one what you're looking for.

3. **Even the person with the best intentions may not remember to call, so take matters into your own hands and follow up with each contact you make.**

10

LANDING THE INTERVIEW

WHAT'S AHEAD

Getting Started

Calling Friends

Before Calling Someone You Don't Know Well

Making the Call

If You're Having Trouble Getting Through by Phone

Making Contact by Mail and E-Mail

Landing the Interview

Putting your squad to work is the next step in this process. With some whom you contact, it will be a two-minute call while they provide you with a name and telephone number or two; with others, the conversation will be more lengthy. A few may even have specific job advice to offer, and it will be worth your time to arrange to meet with them.

A friend of mine who wanted a job in public relations had been given the name of a powerful person in a major agency. After this executive cancelled their appointment several times, she then called out of the blue and invited my friend to lunch. They were to meet at a very trendy lunch spot. The PR person kept my friend waiting for 15 minutes, but during her wait, she bumped into an old acquaintance of the family who heard her story and immediately knew someone who was expanding his public relations department. After following up on *that* lead, my friend got the job.

The moral of the story is, "you never know exactly how this is all going to work out, but if you keep making the right contacts, you'll get the interviews you need to get a job."

To land the interviews *you* need, here's how to ask, what to ask, and what you can expect will result.

GETTING STARTED

In all likelihood, the people on your first list don't have the job that's right for you, but through the names they give you and the names you

---

acquire from *their* contacts, you are going to find your next job. Getting started with this process is a lot like doing a jigsaw puzzle: you have to continually unscramble, sort, and place to make all the pieces fit.

For this reason, when you approach this first "circle of friends," you're not asking for a job—you're asking for suggestions about people whom you can contact to find out more about a particular field or a specific company.

Whether to contact them by phone or by mail should be decided on a case-by-case basis. You'll know right away those whom you feel comfortable phoning (your roommate's brother, your Uncle Stephen, the woman who runs the local chamber of commerce who is a friend of your spouse's). Those whom you're not comfortable phoning should be approached by mail with a follow-up phone call later on.

CALLING FRIENDS

Phoning people you know well is easy. Call each person on your list. Explain what you're doing (job hunting) and the type of job you're looking for. Ask each for suggestions or for a networking referral. There's always someone who can be helpful.

Enter all names and contact information into your notebook.

BEFORE CALLING SOMEONE YOU DON'T KNOW WELL

Have you ever practiced making a phone call? If not, doing a "dry run" will serve you well. Even when you're asking for just a few minutes worth of advice by telephone, you **are** calling people you don't know and asking a favor. You need to be direct, specific, and well-spoken when you call:

- In advance, think about how you want to start out:

  — You need to refer immediately to the person who referred you to the contact;

  — You need to quickly give some credentials so that the person realizes that you're serious:

    "Dr. John Miller gave me your name. I've just graduated from veterinary school, and I've spent four summers working with a vet who specializes in race horses. I'm hoping to get a job at a track or with a stable and would like to speak to you about what you might recommend."

  — In the above example, the person has provided a credential— vet degree—and expressed serious interest in a specific aspect of the work by describing her summer employment. This should provide the contact with enough information to at least keep him on the phone for a few minutes.

- Decide what your opening line is going to be and rehearse it before making the call.

- Though there will be a temptation to blurt out your line as quickly as possible, practice saying it slowly so that it's understandable. If what you've written seems like too big a mouthful, break it up. Plan to make your first statement, and then mention any other points as you go on.

"TO DO" ITEM #21:

Practice making phone calls.

Making the call

- Once you reach the person you intend to contact (keep reading for suggestions on getting through to the hard-to-reach), introduce yourself (as discussed above), and then say, "Do you have a moment?"

- If you've called at a bad time, explain briefly what you need ("Mary thought you could refer me to a few people in my field . . . ") and ask when would be a good time to call back.

- If the person agrees to talk for a moment, explain about your career exploration, and ask if he or she might give you names of people in the industry (or company) who might be helpful.

IF YOU'RE HAVING TROUBLE GETTING THROUGH BY PHONE

- Try calling before 8:30 A.M. and after 5:00 P.M. Even someone with a secretary may answer her own phone at that time, and you'll have long enough to pose your question.

- Befriend the secretary. Get a name so that you can begin to build a relationship. If getting through seems impossible, you might even explain to her why you're calling; she may be able to get your message through—along with a reply.

- If you get voice mail, go ahead and explain why you're calling. Because you won't necessarily receive a return call, you may at least have furthered your progress by letting him know why you're phoning.

MAKING CONTACT BY MAIL AND E-MAIL

Those whom you don't know well or whose schedules are extremely busy will need to be contacted in another way. The friend who gives you the person's name will likely have a suggestion: "You better write first—she's a great person to know, but she travels a lot." Or: "Call Harry, but he's really hard to reach—here's his e-mail address." It's best to follow these clues.

Getting in Touch by Letter

If a formal letter seems like the best approach, then here's what to do:

- State up front who you are and who referred you:

    "Dee Smith suggested I contact you. I am almost finished with my training to become a pharmacist. She thought you might be able to refer me to some people who could help me get a start in the field. . . . "

- Say in your letter that you will follow up by telephone on or after a certain date. Don't be so specific that you'll look disorganized if you don't call at the exact hour you said you would. It's fine to specify a window of time.

- Enclose a resumé. While the person may only skim it, he or she may make a connection or have a brainstorm based on something in the resumé, and this will make it easier to get help.

- Note on your calendar to follow up. Write the person's name and phone number on the "to do" list for that date.

Getting in Touch by E-mail

Those for whom you have an e-mail address may respond quickly:

- Use the subject line to indicate from whom you got his or her name: "referred to you by Sally Stone." This increases the likelihood that the person will open your e-mail without thinking that it's junk.

- State in your e-mail essentially what you would have said on the telephone. Provide a quick description of your situation. Because the person can scan more than he can listen to easily, you can afford to add a couple of sentences that provide a little more background:

> "For the last three years, I've worked for MNO Company which sells machine parts over the Internet as well as in brick-and-mortar outlets. I was one of the designers of their intranet, linking all their traditional stores, and we've tracked a 25 percent increase in efficiency since this linkage.
>
> "I'm now looking to move to a new position. I enjoy the work I'm doing but I would like to apply what I've learned to other types of companies. . . ."

- Then ask for referrals to other people or for those in your industry, "a few minutes of their time."

- Close with something similar to the following: "If you can reply by e-mail, I'd be very appreciative. Otherwise, I'll call you next week." This lets you maintain control—if you don't receive an electronic reply, you'll still be able to follow up by phone.

- Don't send your resumé electronically unless the person replies and requests it. Expecting the person to open an attachment or scan through your background is a burden you don't need to place on anyone—until they ask.

LANDING THE INTERVIEW

Whenever you're contacting someone who works in the industry or company where you might like a job (or anyone who seems like a particularly helpful contact: "Call my Aunt Sarah—she knows *every*-one. . . ."), use your introductory line and then ask if you could "come in and talk to them for twenty minutes." (You'll get a half hour; few book appointments every 20 minutes.)

Explain that you'd like some advice on getting started (or changing jobs) in the industry. By appealing to this person as an expert, you increase your chance of setting up one of your first appointments.

Once you've got your first date on the calendar, you're all set. You've landed your first interview!

KEEP IT SIMPLE

1. **Start getting in touch with your list of contacts.** Ask each for referrals to anyone who could be helpful to you in getting your next job.

2. **Think through in advance exactly what you want to say before phoning any people whom you don't know well.**

3. **Write or e-mail people whom you're not comfortable calling, but plan to follow up by phone.**

11

INTERVIEW PREPARATION

AND HOW TO HANDLE THE INFORMATIONAL "MEETING"

WHAT'S AHEAD

Practice Presenting Yourself Well
Practice, Practice, Practice
The Informational Meeting

When most job seekers anticipate going out on an interview—even the meetings that are merely to learn more about an industry—they feel very nervous:

— "Will I make a good impression?"

— "Will I know what to say?"

— "Will I be able to convince them I'm right for the job?"

And of course, almost everyone imagines *their* worst: "What if I trip on the way in, or spill my coffee, or my mind goes totally blank?"

Rest assured that your concerns are perfectly normal. Virtually everyone feels self-conscious as they begin this process. However, with a little practice and a new way of viewing things, you'll soon find that the process needn't be as daunting as you thought.

PRACTICE PRESENTING YOURSELF WELL

There are several primary elements—making eye contact, having a good handshake, presentable demeanor, and pleasing speech patterns—which can be practiced in advance, and this will make it easier to make a good first impression. The more these habits feel like second nature, the less you'll have to think about them as you start going on "real" interviews:

Making Eye Contact

People who don't look directly at others give the impression of being shifty, flighty, cold, or insincere—qualities you certainly don't want to convey in any type of interview.

The moment you're introduced to someone, you need to make eye contact. Making eye contact, of course, doesn't mean locking gazes with someone—it means speaking directly to a person and not letting your eyes drift all over the room while you're having a conversation. Some people say that focusing on the color of someone's eyes helps you accomplish this task.

Practice good eye contact with friends and family. When your spouse comes in the door, look directly at him or her, and ask about his or her day. When you run into a neighbor, take a moment to talk directly to her. You may find you get a deeper more meaningful answer from everyone with whom you try this, simply because the eye contact—and the fact that you stopped to ask a question—makes you seem very sincere.

You'll soon find that the more you practice, the less you'll have to think about making eye contact. By the time you start interviewing, it will seem totally natural.

The Handshake

A good handshake is firm and friendly. It shouldn't be so firm that the other person's hand hurts afterward, but there should be some substance to it—no one likes the feeling of shaking hands with someone who offers you a limp paw.

Practice your handshake with a friend or family member. Ask for feedback on your grip. When you practice, stretch out your hand to your friend, and practice saying, "It's nice to meet (or nice to see) you, Mr. So-and-so." By using the person's name, it not only establishes a rapport with the person, but it also helps you remember the name as you begin your conversation.

In an actual interview, the interviewer should take the lead. Generally, the person will offer to shake your hand as you enter the office. Occasionally you'll run into someone who doesn't like to shake hands; in this case, the proper thing to do is to nod, say, "It's nice to meet you, Mr. So-and-so," and then proceed with the discussion.

Demeanor

Whether we like it or not, people form opinions of us based on how we look—not so much what we wear, but how we stand (straight with shoulders back? Slouching? Half-straight, half-slouch?) and what kind of an expression we have on our face. For that reason, it's worth working on both.

While it takes a long time and a lot of concentration to change one's posture, there are some simple things you can do that can make a big difference in body language:

- Starting now, stand as straight as you can and hold your head up. This may not give you perfect posture immediately, but it will make you look like someone who feels good about him- or herself.

- Pay attention to your posture when sitting. Don't slouch. You don't want to arrive at an interview and inadvertently slide down into the chair or couch. It may be comfortable to sit that way, but it won't give a good impression to an interviewer who is looking to hire someone who is eager and attentive.

- Facial expression is also an important element of how you present yourself. Unfortunately people tend to get a "tight" look when they are nervous. Work on responding to comments with smiles when appropriate; smiling is a great way to counter tension.

- Demeanor can also be affected by nervous habits. Ask for feedback from friends about anything they notice about you, and work to break them before you start interviewing. Rubbing your chin, fiddling with your watchband, or tossing your hair can be very annoying if done repeatedly.

Plain Talk

- Speak slowly and distinctly. Just as you practiced speaking clearly for making telephone calls, work on this for future interviews as well. Many people speak quickly when they are nervous; remember to slow down so that you can be understood and so that the interviewer isn't reminded of how ill at ease you may feel.

- Avoid inserting "ummm" or "uhhhh" into your sentences or thoughts. Pausing is preferable. If you've fallen into this habit, ask family or friends to help you by pointing out when you're doing it so that you'll have an opportunity to break the habit.

- Don't mumble. It makes it difficult for others to understand you, and you don't come across looking eager and capable. Think before you speak and then <u>concentrate on speaking carefully.</u> After a little practice it won't seem awkward at all.

- Don't swear. Many people are offended by the use of curse words, and it certainly doesn't present a professional impression. By reducing your use of questionable words in day-to-day life, you'll lessen the risk of saying something in an interview.

"TO DO" ITEM #22:

Practice making eye contact; work on a firm handshake; concentrate on posture; and consider how you speak.

By making these habits routine, you'll have more confidence and energy for the actual interviews.

PRACTICE, PRACTICE, PRACTICE

Pretending to go through the interview experience will help you when the moment actually comes:

- Find a friend who will help you practice. If you know anyone else who is job hunting, you can help each other and take turns being in the "hot seat."

- Create a list of questions for the person to ask you. By anticipating questions, you'll be well prepared for most things that will come up in an interview. (To create this list, refer to Chapters 14 and 15 and note those questions that might give you difficulty.) Include on your list everything from the open-ended type of question, "Tell me about yourself" to the personally challenging, "Why would you want to work in a farm town like this?"

- Encourage the person helping you to change the order and create questions of his or her own.

- Start any practice session from the moment you would enter the room and shake the interviewer's hand. This will help both of you take on your designated roles.

- Afterward, ask your friend to critique the interview. What went well? What needs more work? Does he have any suggestions on how you might present yourself better?

- After you've survived a basic practice interview, ask someone (the same friend, or ask someone new) to help you by going through the same drill but to try being abrasive or overly friendly. This will provide you with a different type of interview experience.

"TO DO" ITEM #23:

Ask someone to help you practice being interviewed.

THE INFORMATIONAL MEETING

The next step in building your interview skills is to begin testing them out in a situation that isn't as stressful as an actual job interview. The information-gathering meetings with people whom you want to ask about a particular company or the industry in general are valuable opportunities in their own right, but they are also a perfect time to gain additional experience at presenting yourself well in a formal situation. Here are some suggestions to make the sessions go smoothly:

- Just as you did when networking, you're going to set a specific goal for each informational meeting you're able to schedule. Some of these would be typical goals:

  — "I want to learn more about the industry."

  — "I want some ideas as to how best to present my qualifications for a job in this field."

  — "I want suggestions as to what type of position might be open to a person with my background."

  — "I want the name of someone who might help me get a job within this company."

- Prepare questions so that you're able to use your time well.

- Out of respect for the person you're visiting, do some advance research on his or her company. (Call the person who gave you the contact for a little information about the person you're seeing as well.) "Tell me, exactly what does ABC Manufacturing make?" is the type of question that will hasten your exit from someone's office—if you're going to ask them to share some time with you, you need to know the basics about the business or the company for which the person works. (See the next chapter for information about researching a company.) They shouldn't have to do a complete "what it's all about" lesson for you.

- Take copies of your resumé and your business cards. A copy of your resumé should be presented when you're introduced; by having extra copies you'll have spares in case he or she wants to send it on.

- Just as you will for your real interviews, you're going to dress well and arrive promptly.

- Be conscious of the time. The person has probably set aside 30 minutes for you, and you don't want to overstay your welcome. Respect the fact that this person may have taken time to talk to you but still needs to stay on schedule with the rest of the day's appointments.

- Ask your questions in a businesslike but casual manner. If the person you're seeing takes the conversation in a different direction, and it's productive, skip some of your questions. You can ask them of someone else.

- At the end of your time, bring the meeting to some sort of resolution relating to your goal:

— "I'll be very appreciative of any job leads you can give me . . ."

— "Thank you for telling me about the ABC organization. I'll contact them for more information. May I call you in a month or two if I have any questions?"

— "I'd love to learn more from Mr. So-and-So. May I ask your secretary for the information on contacting him?"

- Afterward, write a thank-you note. If you have not left a resumé, enclose it at this time.

- Conclude with a line about "I'll let you know how everything works out." Then do. It makes them feel a part of your squad, and eventually he or she will feel a participant in your success.

"TO DO" ITEM #24:
Start calling to set up informational interviews.

KEEP IT SIMPLE

1. **Consider your posture, your facial expression, your speech patterns, and your general demeanor.** Work at trying to come across as controlled but relaxed.

2. **Ask someone to stage mock interviews with you.**

3. **Treat the informational meetings you're able to schedule very seriously.** Don't be late, and enter into each session with a specific goal so that you can lead the conversation around to what you need to talk about.

12

FINISHING YOUR HOMEWORK:

COMPANY RECONNAISSANCE

WHAT'S AHEAD

Your Method of Approach

Consider Lifestyle

If You're Interviewing in a New Community

Once an interviewer agrees to see you, you have a lot of work to do. You need to learn what you can about the company before your interview. Doing your homework assures you of two things:

1. **You increase your chance of getting the job.** Remember, the company is looking for someone to solve problems in a specific area, and it's harder to resist an applicant who obviously took the time to "study up" beforehand.

2. **If you are offered the job, you'll be better prepared to assess whether it's the right job for you.** (Getting a job and accepting a job are two different things—if you're offered a job and there's no room for advancement, or you didn't feel you would function well under that particular boss, you may be wise to keep looking.)

The amount of research you can do prior to an interview to some extent depends on how much advance notice you have. Here are some tips on how to go about it.

YOUR METHOD OF APPROACH

- Call and ask for a brochure about the company or a copy of the annual report. (Brochures would be sent out to any and all potential customers; annual reports are for potential investors.) Finding out what the company says about itself is an excellent start. If the business is a local one, ask if you can stop to pick up the information. This gives you an excuse to go into the company and observe. While there, don't rush to leave. Just watching people come out the main door and go into the parking lot may give you a feel for the type of people who work there. (Another benefit to stopping by in person is that it gives you an opportunity to navigate the route and plan out how long it will take when you return for your interview.)

- Check to see if the company has a Web site. A good Internet site will be very similar to thumbing through a company brochure. It should give background on the company along with any current information it's disseminating. Regular press releases as well as specialized information for the Web site are usually posted.

- For general questions about a profession or an industry, try posting a question on the appropriate bulletin board on one of the online services. You will undoubtedly get a good response. Don't write anything too specific. For all you know, the person who is going to interview you may be following the postings online, and you don't want to be embarrassed about anything you posted.

- Call the trade organization for the industry. The organization itself may have information, or the staff may have leads you can follow for learning more about a company.

- Visit the library. A research librarian will be able to point you toward books that should have information about the industry or company in question. Some libraries even have clipping files of articles on area companies, CEOs, and industries.

- If you have contacts who are in the field, call them for background information. People outside the company may know something about the general culture and how the business is doing; people within the company can, of course, be very helpful. Try asking: "I'm interviewing with Bill Smith for a job in marketing. What can you tell me?"

- Contact your school alumni office for names of people who might be helpful. In addition to learning some information from the alumni, you may actually find yourself with a new friend; someone who is in just the right place and will put in a good word for you.

- Also familiarize yourself with the company's products and services. If the product is sold locally, visit the appropriate stores to examine the product line.

- Think through the position for which you're applying. Consider whether there are specific issues involved with the job for which you're being considered. If you hear rumors of cutbacks in a particular department, you'll want to consider whether the cutbacks would affect the department in which you might be working.

As you conduct your research, look for answers to the following questions:

— What is the main focus of the company?

— Is the company a leader in the field?

— What is its customer base?

— What type of companies make up the competition?

— Is the company growing? Cutting back?

— Can outsiders describe a "culture" that is associated with the company? What do insiders say?

— Is the company huge, with all sorts of people working there, or are there fewer employees? In either case is there an identifiable company personality "type"?

— As you gain insight into the company, can you begin to see how your skills and interests would be an asset to the company?

Begin to formulate a case for what you would bring to the company.

• Put all information relating to the company in a file for that purpose. Record your thoughts and the questions you'd like to ask at the interview on a page in the "Interview Preparation" section of your Job Search Notebook.

"TO DO" ITEM #25:

Conduct as much research on each company as you can before the interview.

CONSIDER LIFESTYLE

One young woman who finished law school did her research before looking for a job. She learned that new lawyers in New York were expected to work many more hours than were new lawyers in Los Angeles. Because she was more interested in practicing law than being on any "fast track" for a New York law firm, she did the obvious—she job hunted in L.A. If you sense that the employees at a particular company are more serious about their work—or less serious about their work—than you want to be, keep looking. This is a valid reason for deciding for or against a job.

IF YOU'RE INTERVIEWING IN A NEW COMMUNITY

If you're interviewing at a company that would require you to relocate, anyone doing the hiring will want to be assured that the job is right for you, and he or she will also want to know that you'll be able to create a lifestyle you like as well. No company wants to invest in bringing in a new employee and training him or her, only to have the person leave within a few months, "because living here wasn't what I expected."

- Call the chamber of commerce for information.
- Visit the community's Web site.

- When you arrive in town for your interview, buy and read a copy of the local newspaper and any local magazines that might exist.

- If you're staying overnight prior to the interview, be certain to read the local morning paper before going to the interview.

As you go through the process, consider:

— If you're used to skiing most winter weekends, can you really be happy in Florida?

— If you love the seasons, how do you feel about living in southern California?

— If you hate winter, do you really want to work in Minneapolis?

— If you love seeing theater, how will you feel about a town of 10,000 where the community theater performs only once a year?

— If you like wide open spaces, how are you going to feel in a big city where you'll depend on crowded buses to get around?

— If you relocate, will this bring you closer or farther away from family and friends? How do you feel about this?

Create questions of your own, based on your likes and dislikes. While some jobs may be so wonderful that it's worth trying some place that may not be "made for you," you should still evaluate the pluses and minuses of a particular location.

"TO DO" ITEM #26:

If you would need to relocate for a job, research the community carefully.

Most people who take the time to do their homework and research what life would be like in this new position have already "moved to the head of the class."

KEEP IT SIMPLE

1. **Before you go to an interview, do as much research as you can about the company and about the department where you'll be interviewing.**

2. **Collect brochures, printouts, and annual reports in labeled files.** Note questions you'd like to ask about the business in your Job Search Notebook.

3. **Consider the lifestyle that would go along with a new job.**

13

DRESSING THE PART:

WHAT TO WEAR

WHAT'S AHEAD

The Basics
Special Advice for Men
Special Advice for Women
Hair Care
The Day Nears . . .
Briefcase Essentials
When Travel Is Involved
Help!

While everyone knows it's "what's inside that counts," dressing the part when going on a job interview is more important than some people realize. You don't want to waltz into your interview at an "animal rights" organization wearing a fur coat, nor do you want the law firm where you're interviewing to wonder if you would appear in the courtroom in an open shirt (no jacket), khaki pants, and loafers.

Planning what to wear to each interview is well worth the effort. You'll be taken more seriously and dressing well will make you feel professional about the task at hand—the interview.

THE BASICS

- Every job seeker should have a minimum of two outfits that are suitable for interviews. That way if one is at the cleaners, you can wear the other ensemble.

- The clothing you select should look as expensive as the salary you aspire to make, and your attire should suit the industry to which you're applying. If you're interviewing for an accounting job, your clothing will be more conservative than if you're going to an interview with an advertising agency.

- Each company has its own culture. If you have the opportunity to observe people who work at the company where you'll be interviewing, it will give you some ideas of how you might dress to look as if you fit in. (If all the women tend to favor black, you'll know not to go for a more colorful look.) If you don't have the opportunity to observe beforehand, a basic interview outfit is your best bet for the first interview. If you're called back, you can adjust what you wear for the second visit.

- When you read through these suggestions you may feel you're leaving your personality at home. That's not the case. The purpose of the initial meetings is to convince the employer that you're the person who can solve a problem (job opening) he or she has. You don't want what you wear to be distracting. The last thing you want the person doing the hiring to say as you leave the office is, "Hey, did you catch those huge rings the guy was wearing!" Simple is best.

"TO DO" ITEM #27:

Prepare two interview outfits and have them in your closet and ready to go at all times.

SPECIAL ADVICE FOR MEN

- A suit and tie are a must. Though this may be an additional expense for a student or someone who has been out of work for a time, it is a wise and necessary investment in your future. A few candidates opt for gray slacks and a navy blazer, but do some research in advance to make sure you won't look totally out of place in this more casual attire.

- Select a suit that is traditional in cut and color; blue and gray are frequently worn. It will last you for more than a single season without looking dated. The weight of your suit will depend on the season in which you're job hunting—the best investment is a suit that is light enough to be worn in spring and fall, but not so light that you can't wear it in the winter.

- Your dress shirt should be white or a pale color.

- Choose a conservative tie for almost all interviews. You don't want to be remembered as the guy with the zany tie. Consider what the current fashion is in tie width; a "power red" tie with or without stripes is a nice complement to most suits and is generally appropriate for interviews in any industry.

- Select socks that are long enough that your bare leg doesn't show when you sit down and your pant leg rides up. Buy several pairs of these socks and make certain that you always know where they are in case an interview comes up unexpectedly.

- Black leather dress shoes are your best bet for footwear. If you aren't buying a new pair, make sure your shoes are clean and polished, and have them reheeled if necessary. Shoes that are worn down at the heel can make you look shabby. You'll have no control over how much walking you may do, so be sure your shoes are comfortable.

- Choose a matching leather belt to wear.

- Visit the barber for regular haircuts during the period you're job hunting. Looking trim and well-groomed is an important part of the process.

- If you have a pierced ear or other body piercing that is obvious, remove the jewelry until after you've had an opportunity to observe the culture. If you're applying for a job in advertising, you may already know that a pierced ear is perfectly acceptable, but if you're looking for a job in a law firm or a bank, you'd be well advised not to wear your jewelry until after you've proven your worth to them and been hired.

SPECIAL ADVICE FOR WOMEN

For women, selecting the appropriate attire may seem more complex: Skirt? Pants? Suit? Bright colors? Dark colors? While women do have more options, keep in mind that for the first interview particularly, you can't go wrong with a "safe" interview suit. Here are the basics you should have in your closet:

- A navy, black, or gray suit will be useful. It can be up-to-date in styling; you just don't want it to be so high fashion that you draw more attention to your clothing than your job skills.

- Pants or skirt? In most cases you'll be safest wearing the skirt. Make sure it isn't too short. Put a chair in front of a full-length mirror and see how you look sitting down and getting up again. Test the skirt again by sitting down on a somewhat soft easy chair or couch—sometimes it can be quite difficult getting up and you'll want a little extra skirt length to be able to do it gracefully.

- Consider whether you need a slip and if so, what style. This isn't something you want to discover the morning of an interview.

- Select stockings in an appropriate color—a nude or dark shade is best. Double-check that the color is right by taking your skirt and shoes as well as the stockings into the daylight—colors look different in natural light. Buy several pairs of the stockings and put them away so that you'll know exactly where they are when you need them.

- Shoes should be selected partially based on current style and largely based on comfort. Once you're at the company for your interview you may be taken to various offices or from building to building, and you don't want to be thinking about how much your feet hurt during this time. For this reason, low heels are recommended. Keep them dressy enough to look fashionable but still comfortable enough to walk in.

- Avoid wearing a great deal of jewelry. It's unprofessional, and you don't want all that "sparkle" to convince the interviewer that you don't really need the job. Select a simple necklace and earrings (ones that don't dangle) that are right for your outfit.

- Women job candidates face a dilemma that men don't. If you carry a purse and a briefcase (keep reading for additional advice on briefcases), it can get very unwieldy to manage both when you arrive for an interview. You want to be able to move from place to place comfortably and to be able to shake hands with people whom you meet without doing a lot of shifting. There are three possible solutions:

1. **Select a small clutch-style purse that can be slipped into your briefcase.** If you're taken for lunch, you can ask about leaving your briefcase in someone's office and carry only the purse with you.

2. **Use a slightly oversize tote as your purse and keep relevant papers inside it.** While it will work, this solution can be a tiring one—if you have a good number of papers, your shoulder and arm may ache after a day of interviewing.

3. **A smaller shoulder bag or purse along with a notebook-size leather portfolio for your papers is another solution.**

- If you are carrying a purse, make sure it looks first-rate. Don't use the sports bag that you take to the mall, the gym, or the beach. Purchase a bag that looks businesslike and that looks well with your suit.

HAIR CARE

- Work with a hair stylist to come up with a look that is becoming, easy enough to care for, and will neaten up quickly if you're buffeted by the wind on the way to an interview.

- Get your hair cut regularly so that an unexpected phone call from a company inviting you to an interview the next day won't throw you for a loop.

THE DAY NEARS . . .

- Give your clothes a test run. <u>Try on everything you plan to wear several days before your first interview, and make certain everything looks just right.</u> You may find your jacket needs to be re-pressed or that there are loose threads hanging off the pants. Take care of it now.

- Also preview your clothing for comfort. You won't interview well if the collar is too tight or if the skirt is itchy. Don't assume you'll "get used to it." If anything, anxiety before the interview will make the discomfort worse.

- The weather prediction is for 95-degree heat. What should you do? While you may be tempted to dress down because of the heat, it's important to wear normal business attire. You'll be in an air-conditioned building, and while you may get hot on your way, you can carry your jacket and put it on once you are inside.

- Cologne and perfume are nice but use in moderation. If you over-scent, you run the risk that your interviewer dislikes the smell, or even has a bad reaction to it.

- Don't chew gum, and avoid smoking on or near the premises. (If you're a compulsive gum chewer, find some way to remind yourself to get rid of the gum before you arrive at your destination.)

BRIEFCASE ESSENTIALS

Unless your current one is beaten up or weakens your overall look, you needn't rush out and buy a new one. I prefer soft-sided over suitcase style; it's easier to carry from office to office during the interview process. Select a style that is water-resistant (keeps your papers dry in the rain), closes completely (permits you to look neater than if papers are bulging out the top), and has some interior pockets so that you can easily find what you need without fishing around in the bottom of the case.

Here are the basics you'll want to have inside your briefcase for an interview:

- Your calendar (or palmtop computer) and address book.

- A labeled file folder for all the literature you received about the company.

- A labeled file folder holding your resumé and any other information about yourself you're bringing.

- A business card case that holds your cards. (Women may find it more convenient to carry this in their purse if they are carrying one.)

- An empty envelope for business cards you acquire.
- A tablet for taking notes.
- Pens, pencils, highlighter.
- Some coins for parking meters, tolls, etc.
- Safety pins to hold loose buttons or a hem.
- Women should pack an extra pair of stockings.
- Reading material, in case you're kept waiting for a long time.
- Small medical kit with a simple pain reliever, Band-Aids, antacids, and allergy medication, if necessary.
- Dark glasses and spare glasses, if you wear glasses.

"TO DO" ITEM #28:

Keep your briefcase well-organized with basic essentials, including folders for holding extra resumés, literature, and business cards.

WHEN TRAVEL IS INVOLVED

- If you're traveling to other cities, it's more important than ever that you test out your outfit before leaving. You'll want to make certain everything is just right.

- Create a packing list, noting all the clothing and accessories you need to bring for each interview.

- Women should be certain to pack extra stockings.

- Carefully press each article of clothing before departure, and pack carefully. As soon as you arrive at your hotel, unpack your bag and shake out and hang your outfit. Many times wrinkles will "hang out," however; take a travel iron with you for last-minute pressings, or call the hotel in advance to determine if an iron can be made available to you in the room.

HELP!

- You're called back for another interview, but you only have one outfit you feel absolutely terrific in. Change the small things—your tie, your blouse, a scarf, or your jewelry. The other person is unlikely to remember exactly what you were wearing. What's most important is that you feel comfortable going into round two of the interviews—a very good sign!

KEEP IT SIMPLE

1. **Every job seeker should have a minimum of two outfits that are suitable for interviews.** Wear something fashionable, but not too trendy, and try it out ahead of time to be certain you feel comfortable in it.

2. **Select your shoes carefully.** They should be of good quality and reasonably fashionable, but be sure they're comfortable. If you do a lot of walking, you don't want to have to think about how much your feet are hurting.

3. **If your briefcase isn't in good condition, invest in a new one, and pack it neatly so that if you open the bag in the presence of the interviewer you look as neat and well-collected as any employer would want you to be.**

14

THE

INTERVIEW

WHAT'S AHEAD

Advance Prep
Managing Anxiety
Learning by Observation
Your Arrival at the Office
Interview Protocol
The Art of Good Listening
Conducting Your Own "Interview"
Developing a Connection
As the Interview Draws to a Close . . .
Don't Let Down your Guard
When There Is More Than One Interviewer
When the Interview Involves a Meal
What Does an Interviewer Want?

One day a friend of mine, a calm, friendly gentleman in his forties, told me what happened to him on a recent interview: "The fellow asked me a question, and my mind just went blank—I was nervous when I arrived, but I left feeling so embarrassed. Boy, after that I always practiced before each interview."

Almost everyone has butterflies in his or her stomach as an interview approaches. It's hard not to feel nervous when a potential job is at stake. However, you've taken all the right steps to get to this point, and continuing this measured approach will help you feel calmer and more in control as the next developments unfold.

What's more, an interview isn't a one-way street. In addition to an employer deciding whether you're right for the job, you should also be checking to see if the job is right for *you*. The wise applicant will be scrutinizing the company and interviewing the interviewer at the same time.

By viewing the process as one that is of mutual benefit, you may be better prepared to step with confidence into the interviewer's office.

Besides that, you never know how the situation may develop: Just before I was to get married, I was searching for a new job. I got a call regarding a position that didn't sound very interesting, but my fiancé convinced me to go "for the interviewing practice." During the meeting, the interviewer kept telling me what I already knew—I was wrong for the job. Taking affront at his attitude, I decided to assure him that I had many strengths, and I really could be right for the job—if given a chance. The result? The next day he called to offer me a much better position. When I asked what persuaded him to decide in my favor, he replied: "This other job requires someone who can overcome obstacles—you'll be perfect."

ADVANCE PREP

- Confirm your interview at least a day in advance. During this call you should also:

  — Confirm directions, and if you'll be driving, ask about where you can park.

  — Inquire about the exact location of the office or meeting room. Office complexes and large medical centers can be overwhelming and confusing, and a ride on the wrong elevator can set you astray. Get specific directions if it sounds at all confusing.

  — If there was any confusion or doubt as to the exact person who will interview you, verify with the secretary whom you'll be seeing.

- If you're concerned about timing your arrival, do a test run at the time of day when you'll be going to your interview. (A trip that usually takes 15 minutes may take considerably longer during morning rush hour, or if you discover there is road work being done.)

- If you're interviewing in a different town, get a map and try to do a test run the day before. Otherwise, you'll have to rely on local contacts to advise you on timing. Be sure to pad their estimate with an additional 15–30 minutes. You don't want to be late.

- Above and beyond the time you'll need to allow for travel, build in some "getting settled" moments. You may want to locate a rest room or just have a few moments to feel collected before going into the interview.

- Lay out your clothing, briefcase, and purse the night before. As discussed in Chapter 13, everything you will wear or take with you to the interview should be carefully checked more than a day in advance—you don't want to find you're missing a button or a hem is pulled out just a few minutes before you need to leave for the interview.

- Put several copies of your resumé (in case you find that you are meeting more than one person) into a file folder in your briefcase, and take along some business cards as well. If you have any portfolio items you need to take with you, be certain that everything is in good order.

- Get plenty of sleep. Being well rested puts you in better condition for answering any and all types of interview questions. A stifled yawn may make you appear disinterested.

- If you have a morning interview, set your alarm so that you'll have at least 15 minutes more preparation time than you think you'll need. If you're staying in a hotel, ask for a wake-up call, but bring along a travel clock as well.

- Allow a few minutes to read the newspaper in the morning; you don't want to be caught off-guard by not knowing about a major story that affects the town or the company where you're interviewing.

- If something unavoidable happens and you are running more than five minutes late, call ahead. (This is where a cell phone becomes valuable.) The interviewer may want to reschedule, but if you've been considerate of his/her time and have a good explanation (major snarl-up on the freeway, family emergency), most interviewers will give you a second chance.

- Once you're at your destination, don't relax quite yet. Be certain that you've found the exact location of your interview. Window shopping in any spare moments before your appointment will seem like a terrible error if you then discover that the office you're looking for must be reached through a different entrance.

"TO DO" ITEM #29:

Call ahead to confirm the appointment and to double-check directions and parking.

MANAGING ANXIETY

There are three simple steps that will help you manage your anxiety:

1. **Arrive on time.** Having a few minutes to pull yourself together prior to the interview will make an enormous difference in feeling at ease.

2. **Focus on your breathing.** People tend to breathe more shallowly when they are nervous. By making sure your breathing is normal, you'll feel more comfortable physically.

3. **And finally, one tip to boost confidence:** This isn't just about them liking you; it's also about you liking the company. If you begin to think of the interview as a two-way street, you'll realize that this interview is about choice—you may or may not want to work here.

"TO DO" ITEM #30:

Prepare in advance to ease your anxiety and help you feel more in control.

LEARNING BY OBSERVATION

From the moment you arrive on site, you should be continuing "company reconnaissance." Evaluate: Do you like the people? Does the job sound interesting? Are there advancement possibilities? Is this a place where you would be happy? Or is it at least a good perch (and credit) to have as you prepare for the job you **really** want?

By approaching this as an "assignment" to understand the job and department better, you may find that enthusiasm actually builds for both you and the interviewer as you have a discussion about the job and the company. This, of course, will increase the likelihood of your getting the job.

Here are some of the ways you can begin to acquire the knowledge you'll need to evaluate whether or not this is the job for you:

Start by examining the building. This is the first sign of how a company views itself. Is the layout an open one with offices more or less open to each other? Are there private offices (and what seems to be the pecking order for those?)? How does the support staff seem to be treated? (Offices that don't treat their support staff well may not treat their other employees that well in the long run.)

While you're waiting, assess the culture. Is the receptionist working, or thumbing through a magazine? Are there people who seem to be killing time in the hallways, or are they having animated discussions about work?

YOUR ARRIVAL AT THE OFFICE

- Announce yourself to the receptionist or secretary. She will likely suggest that you sit down and wait while she announces your arrival.

- If she doesn't offer, ask about a coat closet. It is to your advantage to have one less thing to carry.

- Unless you are told that you have a long wait, use your time to observe the office surroundings or thumb through publications that are already out on the table in the reception area. If you pull out notes, papers, or your own reading, you have to manage to put it all back once someone (possibly the interviewer) comes out to meet you.

- If you're kept waiting a long time without an explanation, check with the receptionist after 15 minutes or so. You may have somehow been forgotten.

- When the time arrives for you to go into the office or conference room, someone (the interviewer?) will come to get you. If it isn't the interviewer, be sure to catch the person's name. Knowing an assistant, a secretary, or a colleague of the person may be helpful to you later on.

- If the person offers their hand, use the firm handshake you practiced, and make eye contact.

- After the interviewer greets you, the two of you will shake hands, and most interviewers will indicate where you are to sit. If no indication is given, ask. You don't want to have settled into a chair only to discover that two other people are meeting with you, and you're all going down to a conference room. (Will you not get the job because you sat in the wrong chair? Of course not, but you'll feel more comfortable if these first few moments go by, and you aren't flustered by anything.)

- If you're given a choice as to where to sit, resist the easy chair or couch if at all possible, and select a straight-backed firm chair from which you'll be able to get up and down easily. If your only option is a low-slung or overly soft seat, sit toward the front of the chair (but not so far forward that you look anxious). This will help in appearing alert and prepared for the interview, and by keeping your feet beneath you, it will make it easier to get up at the end of the interview.

INTERVIEW PROTOCOL

By following proper protocol as you go through the interview process, you'll find that you as well as the interviewer will be more relaxed because all the social niceties are going as expected. This alone can give you an edge. Here's what you need to know:

- If you know in advance how long the interviewer has allotted for your interview, it will help you in framing your answers. If you sense he or she is short on time, you'll know to be especially direct in your answers. This will also force you to prioritize any questions you may have.

- From the outset, take your cues from the interviewer. If he takes a phone call in the midst of your appointment, you have no choice but to wait patiently; if he seems to rush through some of the questions while lingering over others, follow that lead. Your ability to tune in to the rhythm of the person may affect the outcome of the interview.

- Most interviewers chat for a few moments to put job seekers at ease. This time for "small talk" is when your knowledge of the community or something that interests you about the industry may be helpful.

- Whatever you chat about, **don't complain about anything.** You may have spent two hours making a 45-minute drive on icy roads, but you need to find a way to put a positive spin on things: "Oh yes, the roads were bad, but I thought ahead and had a great audio-tape (preferably a business title) and was able to listen to it while I drove." With an answer of this type, you've indicated you're not a complainer, you can anticipate a "snag," and you're capable of making good use of what could have been wasted time. (You can grumble about all the terrible things that happened to you once you're with friends and family.)

- Be polite at all times. Rude behavior will virtually guarantee an end to the interview.

- Be enthusiastic without gushing. Those doing the hiring want to find someone who **wants** the job.

- While it is perfectly appropriate to express your opinions when they are solicited, don't argue or refute statements made by the interviewer.

- Wait your turn before speaking; don't finish the interviewer's sentences for her, and don't interrupt when she is speaking.

- Don't rush to fill any silent moments. The interviewer may be considering who else you should see, she may be looking back at your resumé and formulating another question—it's fine if there are quiet moments here and there.

- Don't worry if you need to pause for a moment to frame your own answer to a question. If you need a little time, you can also say something like, "That's an interesting thought." This buys you a few extra seconds while you decide how to answer.

- Don't indicate you've encountered a certain question previously. As far as this interviewer should be concerned, this is the *only* job you've ever wanted, and you aren't interviewing all over town— you're counting on this company to hire you because you really want this job.

- No matter what the question, honesty is always the best policy. Somehow "white lies" always come back to haunt us, so don't risk anything by fudging the truth.

- Observe how the interviewer is doing. If she looks bored or disinterested, consider turning the tables and asking a question or two of your own. By reinvolving the person, you may yet be able to get the interview back on track again.

- If you'll need to relocate for the job, you need to emphasize what you like about the community. Think of something you love about the state of Indiana that you're likely to pursue if you relocate there. Those who are interviewing in major cities might discuss the excitement of the cultural opportunities offered in big cities.

- If the interviewer seems inexperienced, think quickly of the points you'd like to make about yourself and this job, and fill in as you can with illustrations of how you can help the company.

THE ART OF GOOD LISTENING

Listening carefully when you're nervous isn't easy. There's the temptation to be thinking about what may be asked or to be rethinking what you *should have said* to the question just asked. Some of this will get easier with more experience in interviewing, but here are some tips that can help in the meantime:

- Keep your attention focused on the interviewer by maintaining eye contact.

- Listen carefully to what is said and don't answer until you've heard the full question.

- Ask for clarification if you don't understand the question.

- Keep your mind on what's happening currently; there will be time later on to rethink what you wish you had said.

CONDUCTING YOUR OWN "INTERVIEW"

As you continue your evaluation of whether this is the right place for you, look for answers to the following questions as you talk to the interviewer:

— Inquire about specific duties. If you meet others in the company, try to ascertain how you would interact with them if hired.

— What is the particular accomplishment that must be achieved to do this job well? Higher sales? Greater profit? Reduction in costs? (Later you may want to offer some comments on how you would solve this.)

— Does it seem as though you would have the opportunity to learn a lot quickly and grow within the job?

— Evaluate your potential boss. It may not be a great job if you work for someone disorganized or difficult.

— Does the company seem like a fun place to work? Or if it doesn't really seem "fun," is it a good place for gaining terrific experience?

DEVELOPING A CONNECTION

While experience and qualifications count heavily toward your getting a particular job, the quality that generally tips the balance in hiring has to do with personal rapport. Does the interviewer feel that you'll "fit in" to the company? While some connections can only be described as "personal chemistry" between two people, there are some things you can do to lay the groundwork for making a connection:

- Use the interviewer's name during the interview. (He's "Mr. Smith" until he says you can call him "Mark.") This helps create a more personal feeling about your conversation—even if you are having to use "Mr." or "Ms."

- Pick up on the tempo of the interviewer. If you're a tightly wired "Type A" and the interviewer is a relaxed storyteller, work very hard to slow yourself down. If you're going 100 miles per hour and the employer operates at 60, you're going to make him nervous.

- Be attentive and involved in all conversations. Ask questions; express understanding and empathy when you're hearing an anecdote.

- Enjoy any jokes that are told, but don't tell any yourself. Laughter helps everyone feel more relaxed, but the humor itself should come from those already employed by the company. Humor is a very individual thing, and if you tell a joke the interviewer doesn't find funny, he may decide you don't "fit."

- If you're interviewing in a new town, express interest and admiration for the community. This is your opportunity to show that you've taken the time to look into what the lifestyle in this town would be like. You might comment on a new downtown building or a park you admired as you drove into town. Ask a question or two of the interviewer about some aspect of the community that interests you. (If you ask about bike trails and discover that he's not an outdoors person, flip the questioning and ask what he particularly enjoys about the community on the weekends. You can pursue the conversation from there.)

- Be friendly but don't expect friendship. You may have discovered you have a mutual friend or that you both belonged to the same sorority in college. That's good news, but keep your distance. Unless the interviewer suggests an out-of-office lunch or getting together with the mutual friend, remember that you're here for one thing: a job. You want the interviewer to like you well enough to want to hire you, but you don't want to seem overeager or you may scare the interviewer away.

AS THE INTERVIEW DRAWS TO A CLOSE . . .

- Look for signs that the interviewer is trying to wrap things up. Sometimes the interviewer will close by offering you one last opportunity: "Do you have any other questions for me?" Even though you know the interview is concluding, go ahead and ask one or two questions—it would be odd not to. You can't possibly have learned everything about the job and the company in only a half hour or so.

- As the interviewer stands up, you should as well. Extend your hand and thank him or her for the time. Then ask about the hiring schedule if it hasn't already been discussed. Part of your job is going to involve following up occasionally, and you need to know the schedule under which they're operating.

DON'T LET DOWN YOUR GUARD

Once the interview is over, there is a tendency to let down one's guard. Stay high energy until you're off the premises and are sure there are no company employees nearby. If someone speaks to you in the elevator, be positive and upbeat. If a secretary takes you down the hall to meet someone else or if she gives you a tour of the department, be as polite and interested in her as you were with the interviewer. Powerful secretaries may be instructed to report back, and anyone to whom you are cold or distant can certainly make it difficult for you to get your follow-up calls through.

WHEN THERE IS MORE THAN ONE INTERVIEWER

If you're being interviewed for a more senior position, several people from the company may attend. This changes the dynamics of the situation, and there are several tips that will be helpful in sailing through:

- As you enter the room and are introduced, greet each person individually and say his/her name while shaking their hand: "Nice to meet you, Ms. Hanford." This is polite, and it will also help you remember each person's name.

- Group interviews are often held in a conference room. It may be appropriate for you to take notes, and if so, one of your first notes should be to jot down the names of the people whom you've just met. This will help you feel more secure as the session progresses.

- Listen carefully to all discussion, and while you can acknowledge the whole group while addressing a particular question, be sure you make eye contact with the person who asked the question.

- Don't try to outwit the politics of the organization. Some candidates will direct their comments to the person whom they believe has more power over hiring. While impressing the VIP in the room makes sense in theory, you may have made enough enemies by focusing on him that he'll be unable to get the support to hire you.

- If this is a return visit for you, then you have previously learned how the company functions. Use this as an opportunity to remark on how you see yourself fitting in—what you think you could do to help solve their problems.

- After the interview, don't rush out in relief that it's over. Take the time to go back and thank each person separately, calling them by name.

WHEN THE INTERVIEW INVOLVES A MEAL

The good news is they're buying you lunch (they must like you!); the bad news is you have to survive a meal in front of people whom you hope will hire you. Not to worry. You'll get through it with flying colors by thinking with your head, not your stomach:

- Order carefully:

  — Restrict your order to something that won't be messy to eat. You don't want to have to get through the rest of the interview with a splotch on your tie or blouse. If you get the job, you'll have the opportunity to come back and eat spare ribs or spaghetti to your stomach's content.

  — Consider whether what you order will be something you can eat while carrying on a conversation. Most types of pasta (with the exception of spaghetti and linguine) or tuna or chicken salad tend to be easy to eat without having to concentrate on cutting or eating it neatly.

  — Avoid garlic or onion. If you spend additional time at the company and possibly meet new people, you don't want to have to worry about needing a breath mint.

- Don't order an alcoholic beverage unless your host is insistent. If it is difficult to avoid having a drink, order along with the table and then have only a sip or two.

- Follow the other cues set by your host. Have a salad to start if everyone else is; order dessert only if everyone else is.

- Observe your best table manners. Keep your napkin in your lap at all times, and use utensils for all but the most obvious of finger foods (potato chips/carrot sticks/bread). Don't talk with your mouth full, chew on your ice, pick food out of your teeth, or belch!

- This is the perfect time to learn more about the company and your potential co-workers. You'll be viewed as a good conversationalist if you ask thoughtful questions. Inquire about your host's interests. People enjoy talking about themselves, and he or she will appreciate your interest.

- While the conversation will undoubtedly be less formal than in an office setting, don't relax too much. You're still being looked over and off-color humor or getting too personal with those who are interviewing you might not help your cause.

WHAT DOES AN INTERVIEWER WANT?

People who are hiring someone new for the company are looking for someone who is qualified, enthusiastic, and has drive. A company also wants someone who will fit in and be a team player—doing his or her job but also working as an effective member of the unit. After all the homework you've done, if you want the job you have a very good shot at getting it.

KEEP IT SIMPLE

1. **Be prompt!**

2. **The job will go to the person who is best qualified and who also "fits in," so do all you can to establish rapport with the interviewers.** Tune into that person's "vibes," and try to establish yourself as a person with whom it would be easy to work.

3. **From the moment of your arrival at the company to the moment of your departure, consider yourself "on."**

15

CHALLENGING QUESTIONS AND HOW TO HANDLE THEM

WHAT'S AHEAD

Classic Questions
Money, Money, Money
Encountering the Illegal

I once went on a job interview that made me realize the importance of being ready for anything. I was ushered into the office, sat down in the seat offered to me, and the interviewer leaned back in his chair and said, "Well, you're on!" And while I gulped and turned pale, he just waited.

Most of your interviewers will be far more kind than that. They'll make small talk as you come into the room; they'll tell you quite a bit about themselves, the department, and job—partly because they don't know what else to do. However, they will eventually feel compelled to ask some questions, and it's best to prepare for what may come.

Write down any and all questions you think you might be asked, and make notes as to what you think your best answers are. File these pages in the "Interview Prep" section of your Job Search Notebook.

CLASSIC QUESTIONS

When it comes to what questions you may be asked, there are innumerable possibilities. Here are some of the more common ones, along with suggestions on how to handle each:

What are your strengths? (Variations on this may include: "What accounts for your career success?" "What are your major career attributes?" "In what areas are you most effective?" "What do you do best?" "How are you unique from the competition?" "Why should I hire you for this position?")

This is a question for which you're actually well prepared. The positive sentences you wrote about yourself in Chapter 6 and preparing a "qualifications summary" for your resumé helped you sum up much of what you need to say.

The art of answering this question to the best of your ability, however, involves tailoring it to the job at hand. Ask yourself:

— Given what you know of the job, what particular qualities are needed for this position?

— What type of results are going to measure success in this job (cost-cutting, employee morale)?

— What type of problem solving is the most important here?

Then think back to the background material you've prepared about yourself (consult Chapter 6). From this list, pluck the information that sheds the best light on you for this position. Those are the strengths you want to display.

The best way to discuss your strengths is with a story. For example, mention that cost cutting is one of the things you do best, and then provide an example of how you cut costs for your previous employer. The person who is an excellent manager can talk of getting a department to pull together and become a great team for the good of the company.

Remember, too, that there are both "professional strengths" and "personal strengths." Most interviewers will be looking for answers such as the above that focus on positive accomplishments in your career. A few, however, may pursue the "personal" qualities of which you're most proud.

For questions relating to personal strengths, think through the things people say about you and consider which relate best to a job. Some of your best attributes may not be particularly valued in certain careers. For example, "kindness" isn't a quality that is necessary for a computer programmer or most senior executives (it's a nice asset but not a required one). Prompt, diligent, thorough, and tenacious, however, are all qualities that would be very helpful in most jobs. These are the strengths to point out.

What are your weaknesses? (Variations on this include "What part of your work could use the most improvement?" "What three things would you most like to change about yourself?" "What qualities do you have that have stood in the way of career advancement?")

Just because an interviewer asks about your weaknesses, it doesn't mean you have to tell them about every little one! This question deserves careful thought, because while everyone does have weak points, you want to explain them in such a way that they won't prevent you from getting the job. There are two ways to do this:

1. **Choose your weaknesses carefully.** Don't blurt out: "I'm always late and I'm a terrible procrastinator. It's hard for me to *ever* get my work in on time!" Or: "I had trouble getting along with the people in my last job." (Don't think the interviewer is going to blame that totally on the "other people.")

   Just as you did when citing strengths, consider what weaknesses would be perfectly acceptable in this particular job. A department manager can't afford to be "a mess with numbers," but he could be "a little too detail-oriented" for someone who is supposed to be keeping the overall picture in mind. (You're describing it as a "weakness," but anyone knows that "detail-oriented" could also be viewed as "thorough.")

2. **Indicate that you're working to improve the situation.** A person who confesses to having difficulty writing reports can discuss taking a course on business writing in order to improve, or the person who is sometimes "too controlling" can be working hard at delegating and following up only when necessary.

By stating your awareness of a particular weakness and then discussing how you're solving it, you lessen the possibility of the interviewer considering your weakness as a major "fault."

Tell me about yourself. (Variations on this include the "you're on" question I ran into on my own interview as well as "So, why are you the one for this job?" or "Why should I hire you?")

This type of question is actually a golden opportunity to sell yourself. Unfortunately, it usually doesn't seem that way because the interviewer tends to toss it out at the beginning of the interview before you've had the opportunity to get a sense of the situation or the interviewer's style or personality.

Nonetheless, when you go into an interview, be prepared to launch into your selling points if you need to. (And just because the person said, "Tell me about yourself," don't start with kindergarten.) Begin with a bit of background about what interested you in this field and why you want to work at that company:

> "I've always been interested in plants and gardening, and spent all my spare time in college over in the botanical gardens. When I realized I could earn a living at it by becoming a landscape designer,

it was the answer to my dreams. I've done a lot of work in the Southwest where the climate is similar to here. I think your clients will find my work creative, but I'm flexible—if they have something special they care about, I always try to work that in."

With a reply such as this, the candidate has not only given a touch of background but has heavily laced the conversation with strong qualifications: he's very enthusiastic about this type of work; he knows the climate; he's creative; and he understands about client satisfaction.

Where do you see yourself in five years? (Variations on this include "What are your goals?" and "Where do you want to go with your life?")

Your answers in Chapter 4 will give you some of the basic information to present here, but of course, in each interview situation you need to weave the interviewer's company into your plans: "I hope to work my way up in an advertising agency such as this, and I would hope to be in charge of several major accounts in five years' time."

Aren't you a little young for this job? (Variations on this will include: "You don't really have enough experience for this job . . . ")

Energy, enthusiasm, and youth are your assets in countering this question. "I may be young, but I've had a lot of experience doing paid and unpaid work in college, and I can assure you I'll work as many hours as I need to in order to learn this job and do it right!"

If this doesn't work on your first couple of interviews, don't give up—someone's going to understand that everyone needs that "first break."

Aren't you overqualified for this job? (Variations on this include questions about being too old.)

An employer who poses this question is concerned about two things:

— Will you be too expensive for the job?

— Are you set in your ways and won't have the flexibility a younger person might have?

The compensation issue can be addressed in several ways: At the first interview, delay discussion by saying, "I would very much like to learn more about this job and for you to get to know me better before we resolve the financial issue. There may be a way for this to work well for both of us."

At a subsequent interview when it seems likely that you're the candidate of choice, discuss how the benefits you bring the company (dollar savings you can find in the department, or extra tasks you can get done because of your broader experience) will be so much better for the company that you're worth it. Or you may actually be willing to take on a less challenging job for less pay than you received in former jobs, and you might indicate that your situation in life is such that you're not looking for a "big league job" with a huge paycheck at this time.

The "set in your ways" issue can be addressed by indicating the activities you pursue to stay on top of what's going on—the computer course you've just finished, your devotion to your new palmtop computer for scheduling, and your general enthusiasm for learning new things from the younger generation.

What do you like most (or least) about your current company? While it's generally easy to find something complimentary to say about your current situation, you need to navigate any question concerning "what's wrong with your current company?" very carefully. You never know who plays tennis with whom and how word might travel back to your present boss.

There are two possible routes to take with this answer. The first is to indicate that it's not so much a problem with the company but a problem with the lack of opportunities for you there. The other possibility is to choose something very minor to criticize, such as the fact that your department is very small so you don't have the opportunities you might have in a larger company (if you're interviewing at a larger company). Just stay far away from any questions that concern negative comments about particular personalities.

Why do you want to leave your current job? (Variations on this can include a question concerning why you left any of your previous jobs.)

There are very acceptable reasons for wanting to leave a job, so if you encounter this question, you simply need to choose one:

— *Career growth.* You've progressed as much as you could in your current job, but there is no room for upward movement, or you are no longer learning anything new in the position. It is time to move on.

— *Stability of the company.* With all the change in business today, a perfectly valid reason for wanting to move on is to be with a company that is financially sound. You no longer need to worry about whether or not your job will still exist, but working at a company that's in good financial shape is more fun because there is generally money in the budget for the types of projects that help a business grow.

— *Long-term personal sacrifice.* If you have an extraordinarily long commute, or if you're in a job where you work every weekend, or you're on call 24 hours per day with no relief, these are well-founded reasons for wanting a different position. Every job requires short-term sacrifices, so you don't want to seem like a complainer. However, it is fair to describe negative working conditions, and indicate that you're willing to work hard but that your current job took it a bit overboard.

What if you were actually fired? Be honest—a new company may check you out. Instead of saying, "My boss was a jerk," or "I didn't get along with any of the people," find a way to put a positive spin on it. With all the job changes that occur today, everyone understands the "out with the old, in with the new" philosophy of some managements.

There is still the possibility that a potential employer may call to check on you, so if you left the company under very negative circumstances this requires some attention. To circumvent this, think back to the people you knew at your former company: Find someone at the company with whom you got along, and ask if he or she will provide a letter of recommendation that cites your good points and the contributions you made to the company. If your potential employer sees this type of letter in your file, he may be less inclined to check on the situation personally, and you'll be given a chance to make a new start.

How do you feel about working overtime and on weekends? A negative reaction here during a job interview will get you removed from the candidates list, so try an answer that doesn't commit you to working every weekend but doesn't seem uncooperative: "I always try to plan ahead so that I don't get into a crunch with my work, but if a special project necessitates working overtime, I'm always willing to give the extra effort." With an answer like this you've also been able to convey that good organizational skills are something that you value and will bring to the company.

How do you handle criticism? Here, the correct answer is easy. If you show that you can turn it into a learning experience, that should satisfy the interviewer: "It upsets me when I've made some type of error, but I always use the experience to figure out how to do something better. I remember one boss I had was always very nervous before presentations and would sometimes blow up as we prepared the materials for the event. I soon learned that if I delivered everything to him at least three days in advance, we didn't have these problems—he was calm, and I could get his comments without him being upset about anything."

"Do you have any questions?" (Variations include "Do you have any *more* questions?")

Interviewers get tired of thinking of questions to ask you, so they'll often defer to you while they think about what to say next. You absolutely must go armed with some basic questions specific to the company and the position. These questions can range from how some aspect of the business functions to specific questions about what your responsibilities would be if hired. You may also want to inquire about what criterion will be used for hiring.

If the interviewer defers to you again to ask "if you have any more questions," feel free to bring up anything else you want to know, but if 25–30 minutes have elapsed, the interviewer may be using this as a "last call" before ending the interview. At this point, you can certainly ask about when he or she expects to make a decision.

If you really don't have any other questions, you can express continued enthusiasm and interest with this type of reply: "I'll probably think of something on the way home, but I can't think of anything else now. Could I have your business card in case something else occurs to me." This gives you the contact information you need for following up later on.

MONEY, MONEY, MONEY

Don't bring up the subject of compensation at the first interview. Your task for now is to learn as much as you can about the responsibilities of the position and then sell them on how you're the right person for the job. For one thing, almost every company can dig a little deeper in their pockets for the employee whom they **really** want to hire. (Negotiating your package is discussed in Chapter 18.)

If the topic of money comes up ("What kind of compensation do you expect in this job?" or "Would you be willing to take a pay cut?"), try diverting the topic: "I'm really interested in learning all you can tell me about the position, and until I know more, I really can't judge what compensation would be necessary. Perhaps we could discuss that when we discuss my actual employment."

ENCOUNTERING THE ILLEGAL

Title VII of the Civil Rights Act enacted in 1964 made it illegal to discriminate in hiring on the basis of race, sex, religion, or national origin, and the more recent Americans with Disabilities Act assures equal opportunity for disabled job candidates.

While the wise and knowledgeable employer will steer away from questions concerning these issues, you almost certainly will encounter some questions that will give employers information on these topics. "What do you do on the weekends?" may elicit information from you about your marital status or whether or not you have children. Some candidates have encountered direct questions such as "Do you attend church?"

Technically, an employer can *ask* whatever he wants to; he breaks the law if he uses that information as a reason not to hire you: "She's too involved with her kids. She won't be available to work overtime" would be an illegal reason not to give you the job.

So what should you do if you encounter a question that requires personal information? Use your judgment. There's no doubt that the interviewer has placed you in a predicament: If you don't answer the question, you stand a good chance of offending him; if you do answer the question, you're giving personal information that you really shouldn't have to provide.

The best course of action is to do what makes you comfortable. If you don't mind revealing that you're married with children, you can answer the "weekend" question in such a way that it can't be used against you: "I enjoy spending the weekends with my family, but my husband and I are very lucky—he has a flexible work schedule, so if I ever need to get work done on the weekends, I know he's there for me."

If you don't like the tone of a question or feel as though the interviewer has overstepped proper bounds by asking about your religion or sexual orientation, you needn't answer the question. If this type of behavior is standard for the company, you wouldn't want this job anyway. Move on to the next interview.

THE INTERVIEWER ASKS A QUESTION YOU CAN'T ANSWER

While a job candidate sometimes decides to "make something up" so that she'll still get the job, honesty is always the best policy. Instead, try an answer like this:

"That's a very interesting issue, Mr. So-and-so. I've never encountered it in my current position, but if that's the type of thing that can come up here, I guarantee you I'll develop a plan for handling it."

THE INTERVIEWER CHALLENGES YOU

During the course of the interview, you may make a statement with which the interviewer takes issue. Don't lose your cool! Keep in the back of your mind that she may be putting you through a test to see how you react when placed in a negative situation or put under pressure.

Listen carefully to the arguments put forth by the interviewer, and then voice an opinion—respectfully. You may decide the person has a valid point, or you may want to acknowledge the person's point but state why you see it differently.

THE INTERVIEWER SAYS SOMETHING AND YOU STRONGLY DISAGREE

The way you handle this partly depends on the type of job for which you're applying. If the position in question is for a support staff job where you'll do your work and won't have a lot of interaction after this, then you'd be wise to let the issue go. If, however, you're applying for a management position, you need to take a stand; no company wants a "wimp" in their middle- and upper-management slots.

WHAT TO DO ABOUT ODDBALL QUESTIONS

There are many variations on the "If you could be . . ." question, and you may encounter some. A med school student was once asked about what part of the body he would like to be; a person interviewing for a management job was asked to speculate on being some type of animal.

Don't let this fluster you. The interviewer has either run out of questions or is testing to see how quickly you can react when thrown a "curveball."

Take a moment to consider the question (they can't possibly expect you to be prepared for this one), and then try to think of something that would exemplify your best work qualities. The med student might mention being an eye, because of the vision it would

---

give him for his work; the management person might opt for being a beaver, a hardworking, diligent animal who can make a complex plan and execute it.

Then don't look back. It was an odd question, and by answering it, you've proven that you can think on your feet. If they're not going to hire you because you said "eye" or "beaver," then you probably wouldn't like the job anyway.

A MBUSHED!

So what happens when you're put on the spot? The interviewer can ask any one of several questions that can be embarrassing or terribly difficult to answer: "Rate yourself on a scale of 1–10." "Haven't you been out of work for quite a time?" "Tell me what you didn't like about your last boss?"

Refusing to answer the interviewer's questions is a poor idea, so the best tactic is to smile and act unperturbed. Then do what you can to finesse a decent answer. With one exception, the examples given above can be answered without sticking your foot in your mouth. The one question of which to beware is the one concerning your previous employer: **Never trash anyone or any job from the past. You never know what will come back to haunt you.**

AUDITIONS BUSINESS-STYLE

Depending on your profession, you may be asked to perform a "test" while at your interview. A copywriter might be asked to create an ad, a graphic artist might be asked to execute a design. While there's nothing "fair" about this, the more you take it in stride the better you'll do. In most cases what they're really testing is your ability to perform well under pressure.

Don't fret or make excuses. Just go ahead and take a stab at what they've asked you to do. If you can block out the pressure you're under, you may even be able to enjoy it—that alone may improve the quality of the work.

HOW TO DEAL WITH THE "WHAT I SHOULD HAVE SAID" FACTOR

Inevitably you'll be asked a question that makes you uncomfortable or that you don't quite understand. You try to answer it, but as the interview goes on, you keep thinking back to other ways you could have dealt with the question. Rather than leave the interview full of regret for what you "should have said," try this: "Excuse me, I'm not certain I fully answered the question you asked earlier about _____. I should have explained _____."

The fact that you had the presence and the clarity of mind to try to revisit an issue will get you points, and the best part is you won't leave feeling regretful that you "blew the interview."

KEEP IT SIMPLE

1. **Prepare for being asked all types of questions.** Think through what you should say, and ask someone to rehearse the answers with you.

2. **Regardless of the questions, stay calm and unruffled.** Some of them may be designed to see how well you think on your feet.

3. **The types of questions asked you will help you formulate your feelings about the company, so even the difficult ones provide you with information you need when deciding if this is the job for you.**

16

TURNING AN INTERVIEW INTO AN OFFER:

FOLLOWING UP

WHAT'S AHEAD

First Things First
The Postinterview Evaluation
Building a History

So your interview is over. You go home and wait to hear from the company, right?

Not at all. You now have two important tasks ahead of you:

1. **Learning what you can from the experience so that any future interviews will be even more successful;**

2. **Staying uppermost in the interviewer's mind.**

Here's how:

FIRST THINGS FIRST

- Promptly send any additional information the interviewer requested.

THE POSTINTERVIEW EVALUATION

The next step is making notes about your visit so that you'll be able to re-create the good parts of this interview and improve upon the weaker aspects of it. Keep these notes in the "Interview Preparations" section of the notebook so that you can review them later.

- Write down what went particularly well. When you're having trouble getting up the energy for a future interview, reading this section will give you an instant "evaluation"—even if it's you getting to talk about you!

- Write a reminder of anything you felt could go better. ("Concentrate on catching names. Repeat them after the person is introduced.") Consider whether there were any "trick" questions, if any questions tripped you up or made you feel uncomfortable.

BUILDING A HISTORY

Even after you've interviewed for a job, the actual process of *getting* the job can take a few days or a few months. Keeping a careful record of what transpired each time you were in contact with the company will help you continue to amass a case for why you're the right person for the position.

- Make quick notes of the sequence of events—did you get a tour? Did you visit someone else in another office? Did three additional people join you? As you go on other interviews, you'll find the experiences tend to blur. This type of note taking will help you remember each situation more clearly.
- Write down the names of the people you met. If you picked up business cards, this will be easy; if you don't have anything in writing, call the secretary or operator to get exact spellings. Don't risk misspellings even in your notes; you may continue the error when writing to the person—a big mistake.
- Note down your impressions of these people.
- What was appealing about the job? Now that you've got some distance on the experience, what didn't sound so wonderful?
- What company goals did you learn about, or in what departmental project did they expect to involve you? The answers you write here will be key to following up.
- File this paper in the "Follow Up" section of your notebook.

KEEPING YOUR NAME ON THEIR MINDS

- Send thank-you notes to any and all people you met at your interview, **and do so within 48 hours of the interview.** A good thank-you note goes beyond: "Thank you for seeing me today. I'd really like the job." To create a "selling" thank-you note, you need to remind them of the interview, the discussion, and what you have to offer the company:

> Dear Mr. Jones:
>
> I really enjoyed meeting you and Ms. Taylor yesterday. It was fascinating to hear about the different marketing projects undertaken by The Jones Agency, and I would really like to be a part of it.
>
> I know you're working hard to produce the concert series for the DEF Account, and I think my organizational skills and experience at producing events for GHI Company are tailor-made for reducing pressure in meeting the approaching deadlines.

If the job were to be offered to me, I would give notice immediately and try to start working as quickly as possible so that the project can keep moving along.

I'll touch base when you return from your trip to see if you're close to making any sort of decision.

Thank you for seeing me. Your agency is so dynamic that it would really be an exciting place to work.

Sincerely,

[Your name]

- The above letter goes beyond a basic thank-you by restating a need that has been expressed by the employer, and then reminding him how you can help solve it. The letter also keeps control in your court by stating a time when a follow-up call will be made.

- Thank others as well. If you had more than a passing interaction with the secretary or assistant, add that person to your thank-you list (if it took several phone calls to finally schedule the interview, if he or she took you on a tour of the premises, if he or she was responsible for getting you from office to office . . .).

- Should you thank by letter or by e-mail? It depends. *Send e-mail:*
  — If time is of the essence, go electronic. If the interviewer expects to make a decision within the next few days, you want your message to get to him or her fast.

— If you're applying to a technology firm or any other type of company whose roots are firmly in the future, thank by e-mail. The interviewer would probably be quite stunned (and it might even work against you) if you didn't.

Otherwise, send a letter: There are definite advantages to a piece of paper that can be attached to your resumé or something that gets more than a cursory on-screen glance.

• Based on what you learned about the hiring schedule, set a date on your calendar for following up.

"TO DO" ITEM #34:
Send thoughtful thank-you notes to all whom you met.

MAKING THE FOLLOW-UP PHONE CALL

The date has come to follow up. What do you do?

Difficult as it is to make that phone call, you do have to do it. Here's how to make it easier:

• Rehearse exactly what you're going to say once you're speaking to the interviewer.

• If you've befriended the secretary or assistant, you're already ahead of the game. He or she may put you through quickly or give you some information as to when to call back. Your first priority is to speak directly to the person to try to renew any positive feelings that occurred at the interview.

- If the secretary indicates that the boss tries to return all phone calls, then you can leave a message for him, but don't do so until you know you'll be relatively easy to reach.

- Try the phoning techniques offered in Chapter 10. Call before nine, during lunch, or after five in an effort to reach the person directly.

- While making personal contact is ideal, it's sometimes very difficult to reach some people. A carefully thought-out voice mail message about why you're phoning at least brings your name to his or her attention; a good secretary or assistant can also serve as messenger if necessary. The benefit to leaving word with a helpful secretary is that she is likely to keep you in the loop as to what's going on.

"TO DO" ITEM #35:
Keep following up.

STAYING IN TOUCH

- If the hiring process at a particular company seems stalled temporarily, find ways to stay in touch.

1. **If you know anyone in the company, try to schedule a lunch so that you can keep abreast of what's happening.**

2. **If you know anyone who knows the person who interviewed you, talk to them about putting in a good word for you.**

3. **If you come across a news article that relates to something discussed in the interview, send it to the person whom you met.** Or go to the library or on the Internet and pull up information that would be germane to what was discussed. Go back to your notes and think about what you might do to prove that you're capable of "being part of the team."

4. **If you read good news about the company, clip out the article and send it.** Your accompanying note can restate how exciting it would be to be connected with this type of company.

YOUR RETURN VISIT

You're unlikely to be hired on the basis of one interview, so the next piece of good news would be an invitation to return to meet more members of the staff. To prepare, reread all your previous notes:

- Refresh your memory regarding the names of the people you have already met. Recalling everyone by name is very impressive.

- Review what the company's needs and goals are so that you can remind them how well you would fit in.

- Read through any other notes about what was said or what happened. That way you'll be mentally ready to advance your cause by reemphasizing points that were made.

- Consider what to wear. Unless you were over- or underdressed for the previous interview, there is nothing wrong with wearing the same outfit with some variations in blouse or shirt color and for men, putting on a different tie. Your interview will go well if you look nice but feel comfortable.

- At this interview you are likely to be introduced to even more people who will "vote" on whether you are the person for the job. Keep in mind all the techniques you've learned (making eye contact, being enthusiastic about the company, asking thoughtful questions) so that you'll continue to be "the lead candidate."

- When this interview is over, ask again about when a decision might be made. Then proceed to follow up in the same way discussed earlier:

1. **Make notes about the experience;**

2. **Send a thoughtful thank you to all whom you met;**

3. **Keep following up by telephone or by sending relevant information to them by mail—just as if you were on the team.**

THE IMPORTANCE OF PERSISTENCE

It's hard to remain optimistic and enthusiastic about a job when you're faced with calling again and again, but consider this: Some employers actually design the process so that you have to follow up more than once. That way they get the sense of which applicants really care about the job and which frustrate easily. Don't call so often that you're a pest, but do keep calling.

WHAT NOW?

Throughout this entire process you ought to be moving full speed ahead on pursuing any and all other job leads. Until you've actually been hired, you can't afford to count on **any** job coming through. You never know when a company may decide to reduce its headcount or when the person doing the hiring moves to another job.

KEEP IT SIMPLE

1. **Create a way to remember exactly what was said at each company by recording your thoughts and feelings about the company after each interview.**

2. **Find ways to keep in touch by sending in appropriate ideas or relevant clippings with a note attached.**

3. **Be persistent.** Jobs are often lost because of lack of follow-through.

17

JUMP-STARTING YOUR JOB SEARCH

WHAT'S AHEAD

Keep Networking and Learning

If you just missed a couple of job opportunities, it's hard not to be discouraged, but it's important to keep going. If you continue an organized pursuit of your job, you're going to find a position that's right for you.

To keep up the momentum, here's what will help:

KEEP NETWORKING AND LEARNING

- Maintain your contacts, even at the jobs where they've recently filled the positions. The candidate hired may not work out, and they may be looking for you sooner than you would expect. Also, you may have made a contact at the company who liked you but for some reason you weren't quite right for that particular job. If you stay in touch, he or she may hear of something for which you're better suited and you may get that position instead. (If you felt very comfortable with the people at the company, ask for feedback as to why you didn't get the job. The other person may have had stronger credentials or may have been the boss' nephew. Finding out will ease your mind.)

- Make a proposal. If you learn that a company still hasn't hired anyone, offer to solve some of their problems on a part-time basis. One company lost the funding for a full-time position for which they had been interviewing candidates. When one of the applicants learned this news, she counterproposed with a way to do some of the tasks part-time, and the company hired her on a per-hour basis. In less than a year she was hired full-time.

- Sit down with one of your mentors or support group members and review with them your next plan of attack. By gathering support from others, you will feel energized, and if you run into hurdles, you'll have someone to call who can help you devise a way to overcome these temporary obstacles.

- Sit down with your notebook, and turn to the "People" section. Go through all the names you've gathered over the past few months. Get in touch with those who were encouraging but didn't have anything at the time. Their situation may have changed by now, and they may have heard of something that will be helpful.

- Keep your spirits up. Particularly if you're not working right now, it's important to stay involved:

  — Exercise;

  — Eat healthily;

  — Maintain a schedule; too much free time can lead to "over-thinking" your situation, so structure your time carefully. Spend part of the day on the phoning and paperwork involved in your job search and then continue to network later in the day.

- Volunteer in your field of interest. Even if you're currently employed, there may be a way to devote time on Saturdays or in the evenings to learning more about the field as well as making additional contacts.

- Add to your skills. If nothing is coming through for you right now, take a night course on a topic that will be helpful in your career.

KEEP IT SIMPLE

1. Stay in touch with all your contacts, including those at companies where they have just hired a new person.

2. Maintain your schedule—keep working at your job search, but make time to exercise and to stay out in the world meeting new people.

3. If you keep at it, you will find the job that is right for you.

PART FOUR

YOU GOT THE JOB!

18

YOU'RE HIRED!

WHAT'S AHEAD

Confirm that the Job is Right for You
Consult Your Squad
Another Company Still Beckons
What's to Negotiate?
Negotiating
Saying "Yes"
Saying "No"

At last you get the call. You're told that you have the job, what it will pay, and when the company would like to have you start. What happens now?

Fight your urge to respond, "I'll take it!" Instead:

1. **If this is absolutely, definitely the job for you, you still needn't confirm that you're 100 percent on board yet—there's still some negotiating to do.** The more senior you are or the more specialized your skills, the greater the likelihood that you'll be able to negotiate salary. But even if the starting pay isn't negotiable, you have the right to hear about the benefits package before accepting the offer. In this case, a good answer would be: "Terrific. I'm really thrilled with this opportunity, but before I give you a definite 'yes,' is there someone who can explain the company benefits program to me?" This way you've given the indication that you're on board, but you've stated that you expect a fair deal out of it. And if the benefits aren't enough to make the salary acceptable, you, of course, still have the option of turning down the job.

2. **If you're not quite sure about the position, by all means ask for time to think about it:** "Thank you so much for calling. It sounds like an interesting offer, and I'd really like to consider it. Could I call you back _____ (in two days' time) to let you know?" If you have questions about something specific—whether it's compensation or job responsibilities—ask if you can speak to someone about it: "I'm a little unclear about one area of my responsibilities; do you think Mr. _____ would see me again to tell me a little more about this?" In all likelihood, you'll have that meeting.

Here's what to do next.

CONFIRM THAT THE JOB IS RIGHT FOR YOU

Even for the job that seems perfect, go back through all the notes you made after your interviews and think about the following:

- Are you excited about the job itself, or is it a means to an end? (If it's a means to an end, is there a logical way to grow within the job or to move on from it later on?)
- Do you like the idea of what you'll be doing day-to-day?
- Were you comfortable with the person to whom you'll report?
- Do you like the people with whom you'll work?
- Is there a good learning opportunity in this position?
- Will the job improve your long-term career prospects?
- Will the job affect your personal life positively (better financial package, meeting nice people, pleasant atmosphere) or negatively (long commute, late nights, no time for friends or family)?
- Will you fit in and benefit from being part of the culture?

"TO DO" ITEM #36:

Review your notes about the company so that you can evaluate the pluses and minuses of the job.

CONSULT YOUR SQUAD

Call those members of your squad who are most up-to-date on your career progress:

- Explain the job to them. Ask if they see any downside.
- A good friend will hear it in your voice if your feelings are mixed. Talk it out with your friend. If he senses you have some concerns, the two of you will likely be able to assess what the problem is. The solution may be to call back for more information, or it may be to say "no."

ANOTHER COMPANY STILL BECKONS

If you were really hoping to work for Company A and Company B offers you a job, pick up the phone. This is the perfect opportunity to see if there's any way to maneuver for yourself to get the job offer you really want.

Explain the situation and ask your contact where they are in the hiring process. You'll get a clear idea whether they're heartbroken at the thought of losing you. (If they aren't, this puts Company B's offer in a whole new light.) If they do still seem interested, discuss timing. Maybe you can get them to move a little more quickly with their offer.

If they're not willing to change their schedule, you face the possibility that you may need to say no to Company B even without the offer you want from Company A.

There's a risk involved, but if you're lucky it will all work out. Your loyalty will certainly boost your stock with them.

WHAT'S TO NEGOTIATE?

Your salary is just part of your compensation package. When you get a job offer, here are some of the other benefits that should be discussed and/or offered to you:

- *Insurance Benefits:* No matter how young and how healthy you are, you need health insurance. A broken wrist, minor outpatient surgery, or a single night in the hospital can really begin to add up to major expenses. If the company does not offer a health insurance package as part of your compensation, phone around and see what it will cost to purchase your own plan. (Check with your insurance agent but also call any professional organization to which you belong. As a membership benefit, some offer group rates to their members who don't have health insurance.) Whatever it will cost you to purchase your own health insurance should be subtracted from the salary they've offered you. If this research takes some added time, call the person who offered you the job and explain that this is a major concern, and you're trying to find out whether or not you could afford to pay for your own insurance.

- *Retirement Plans:* The younger you are, the more likely you are to think this isn't so important, but think again. If you start to put away money for your retirement early in your career, you can put away less and have more by the time you retire. Saving for later years (particularly in tax-deferred IRAs or 401k plans) is one of those things that really pays off. While it's possible to save on your own, the choice of having savings deducted from your paycheck by the company offers a self-disciplined way to "make that payment first." Some companies match or partially match employee contributions to 401k plans, and this is definitely a long-term benefit worth having.

- *Certain Expenses:* If you're expected to relocate, most companies offer to cover costs if they really need you for the job. Some will even buy your house from you if you have difficulty selling it prior to relocating. If they haven't offered this, it's certainly something to ask for.

- *Bonuses:* Some companies offer signing bonuses, others offer annual bonuses; some have both. Talk to other employees and find out how bonus payments are calculated and how regularly they are paid. (You'll pay taxes on the money whether it's in salary or paid as a bonus.) If you accept the job and are counting on the bonus to live on, it will be a rude awakening if there's a year when bonuses aren't paid. No matter how wonderful the annual bonus offer, it's better to get it in salary.
- *Other Benefits:* If you compare notes with friends, you'll hear of a wide variety of benefits. (See the next section for suggestions on perks you might ask for.)

"TO DO" ITEM #37:

Evaluate both salary and benefits when you consider whether or not the compensation for the job is fair.

NEGOTIATING

Whether or not there is any room for negotiation depends entirely on the situation.

— If your type of expertise is in short supply, there's always room for negotiation because the employer knows that if he doesn't hire you, the next company will.

— If they've wined and dined you and really seem to want you for the job, you can negotiate.

— If you're new to the employment scene and don't yet have skills or expertise that make you "irresistible," you have less room for negotiating. Your day to command the price you want will come. However, remember there are other smaller things you can negotiate— if you'll drive for the job, ask for a car allowance, for example.

When negotiating:

• If you're uncertain as to the fairness of the salary, go on the Internet. There are a growing number of Web sites that give salary survey information; other sites will analyze your offer for a fee. If you're running your own comparison against posted salary surveys, remember to take into account the cost-of-living differences in various parts of the country. You can afford to work for slightly less in parts of the country where the cost of living isn't as high as the major metropolitan areas or the East or West Coasts.

• If you'd really like the job, but want more money, open the negotiation by asking for more money, but keep your requests in line with what was offered. The price the company has put on the table when they set your salary is likely not the final offer, but they don't intend to pay double the figure mentioned either.

- If you sense the salary increases in the negotiation are coming to an end, consider any benefits that you'd like that might help compensate for the salary it looks like you'll be accepting. Some non-traditional perks that have been negotiated include club memberships, extra vacation time, a compressed workweek, flexible summer work schedules, tuition reimbursement, zero-interest rate loans for graduate work, legal assistance, adoption assistance, a manager incentive program, long-term disability insurance, temporary housing for new recruits, and employee discounts on products. Some employees are asking for an earlier date for their first performance review, giving them the opportunity to negotiate for more money sooner than would have happened otherwise.

- If the salary is low, but there are other factors that make the opportunity attractive to you, consider asking if you can freelance or take on other work occasionally. If this is agreed to, get it in writing.

SAYING "YES"

If you're ready to accept the job, call back and thank the person and express your enthusiasm for the job. Also:

- Ask for a job offer letter that puts everything in writing: the position, the salary and benefits, as well as the start date in writing.

- Don't quit your current job until you've got that letter in hand.

SAYING "NO"

Particularly if you're unhappy with your present job or currently unemployed, it can be very difficult to turn down a position, but you don't want to make a commitment that you'll regret in two months. If the job isn't right, there's no reason to think you'll easily be able to move on or move up, or if the pay just isn't acceptable, you need to turn them down. There's always the slight possibility that they'll "sweeten the pot" with more money or some other enticement, but don't count on it.

- Call the person who phoned you; you owe this person the courtesy of a personal reply.

- State your anguish over having to say "no," but explain your reasoning in a positive light: you're looking for a job with more growth potential; you've always had your heart set on working _____ (different setting); you need to make more money.

- It's a small world, and you did a lot of networking in landing this job. You may want or need to get in touch with some of these people another time, so be polite and indicate that you'll let him or her know where you will be working in the future; maybe there will be an opportunity for staying in touch.

- While you may feel both depressed and relieved after making this call, just remember, if you landed one job offer, you'll get another.

KEEP IT SIMPLE

1. **You don't have to say "yes" or "no" right away when you get a job offer.** Thank the person who called you, and give them a time when you'll get back to him or her.

2. **Consider how the job will affect you.** Will it be interesting? Is it compatible with your lifestyle?

3. **Keep in mind that there should be a package of benefits in addition to the salary offered.** Take time to understand what they are worth.

19

GETTING YOUR JOB OFF TO A GREAT START

WHAT'S AHEAD

Say Thanks

Review Your Goals

Be a Quick Study

Don't Whine or Complain

Stay Current

The Organized You

Celebrate

You've worked hard at looking for the right job and landing an offer. Now that you've got what you wanted, here's some advice to make certain that you maximize all the opportunities that are there.

SAY THANKS

- Once all the negotiations are finished and you have your job offer letter in hand, let the person who hired you know how truly excited you are about coming to work for the organization. While a situation can sometimes become a bit tense when you're working out final details, it's important to reaffirm your commitment to the job when the negotiation is finished.

- Many people helped you on your way from where you were to where you are now. Take time now to call, write, or e-mail any and all who helped you. Call your Aunt Minnie who suggested you contact the man who told you about the woman who was looking to hire someone; write a letter to the gentleman who set up the interview. Also thank those whose leads didn't directly result in this job but whose encouragement and contacts helped you along the way.

- Go through the "People" section of the notebook and add to your telephone directory any names of people with whom you expect to stay in touch.

"TO DO" ITEM #39:

Say thank you to all who helped you throughout your search.

"TO DO" ITEM #40:

Enter into your telephone directory those people with whom you plan to stay in touch.

REVIEW YOUR GOALS

- Turn to the "Goals" section of your notebook and read through the goals you set for yourself. Which can be crossed off? What new goals should be set now that you have this major goal behind you?
  - — What do you hope to learn from the job?
  - — Where would you like to be a year from now?
  - — Should you be investigating any type of additional education in order to enhance your job skills?
  - — Are there organizations you should join for professional networking?

- Make a new list of short- and long-range goals. Write on your calendar a date six months from now when you ought to review them again.

- Create a "Job" file and put in it all the information that pertained to your job search, including your goal sheets, your resumé, the pages from your notebook listing relevant organizations, and the names of people who helped you.

- Put your Job Search Notebook on an upper closet shelf. You're not going to need it soon, but there may come a day when you will be starting a new job search and will want to refer to it again.

> ## "TO DO" ITEM #41:
> **Update your goals sheets and set new goals.**

BE A QUICK STUDY

On a practical basis, try to learn what you can so that you'll fit in with the culture:

- Find out the stated work hours and the actual work hours.
- Observe what people wear to work.

- Ask about what happens at lunch. Do people go out in groups, or do they bring their lunches to eat at their desks, or is this a time for client entertaining?

- Ask for and look for learning opportunities. Whether there are formal training programs to attend, or whether you can shadow someone for a day, try to learn as much as you can about the business so that you'll understand how your responsibilities fit in as a part of the whole.

- As you settle into your job, you have three groups you need to begin to learn about and understand:

  — **Your boss.** During the job search, one of your tasks was to evaluate what it would be like working for this person. If you've done your homework, then it shouldn't be too difficult to gain an understanding of this. Always remember that in the work environment, your single most important goal has to be pleasing your boss and making him or her look good. If you accomplish that then you'll be viewed as an important member of the team.

  — **Your co-workers.** There are a lot of politics that go on in companies. As a new hire, you want to do the best you can to assess the company culture and pick up on the "vibes." If there's an antiboss group, don't go to lunch with them too soon. You want to align yourself with those whose goals are the same as yours: helping the company perform as best it can at whatever goals or challenges are put before you.

— **The clients.** Who is more important than a client? Only your boss, if he suddenly needs you. Get to know as many clients as you can and do your best to serve them. That's going to make any company management happy.

DON'T WHINE OR COMPLAIN

If you're upset, talk to your spouse, or call one of your mentors. Whine and complain to that person for a few minutes, and then come up with a strategy to make things better. The last thing you want to do when starting a new job is whine or complain or gossip about people in the company.

If you're able to vent to an outsider and devise a way to solve any problem, you'll find that settling in to the job will be much smoother.

STAY CURRENT

Now that you're employed in the profession you wanted, it's more important than ever to keep up with everything from the daily newspaper to the professional journals. Set aside time for reading on a regular basis so that it will be clear that you're willing to go above and beyond to do this job.

HE ORGANIZED YOU

You've run an organized job search, and you've learned that being organized is entirely possible. What's more, the results have been successful. As you start your new job, remember many of the organizational skills you practiced during your job search. Here are ten reminders that will come in handy on the job:

1. **Write down everything in your calendar or day planner; don't expect yourself to remember appointments or phone numbers.**

2. **Set priorities so that your more important work gets done first.**

3. **Make appointments with yourself (just as you did for running your job search) so that you have the time to focus on major tasks.**

4. **Break major projects down into manageable steps.**

5. **Keep a running list of "to do" items and build your daily task list from this Master List.**

6. **Guard against interruptions.** As you settle into your new job, you'll have to find out when you need to be available and when you can get work on projects that require more concentration.

7. **Don't pile!** Set up a simple filing system—the "Action" files you've already created will still be useful, and besides the company filing system, you'll still want to keep some files of your own.

8. **When you're in the midst of a particularly hectic day, start asking yourself, "What needs to get done? What can wait?"** Any items you weren't

able to finish that day can be slipped over to the next day's "to do" list.

9. **Manage incoming information efficiently.** From regular mail to e-mail, office workers today need to process what's coming in as quickly as possible or the backlog that builds up is truly overwhelming.

10. **At the end of the day, take ten minutes to clear off your desk and plan out your next day.** You'll be surprised at how much easier it is to get started in the morning when you walk into an organized environment.

"TO DO" ITEM #42:

Stay organized!

CELEBRATE

Whether it's a night out, a weekend away, or a full vacation, take time to enjoy the successful conclusion of your job search.

KEEP IT SIMPLE

1. **Absorb as much as you can about the culture of your new work environment (the hours, the dress, the use of the lunch hour, the habits of the staff) so that you'll fit in as quickly as possible.**

2. **Don't complain about anything to your new co-workers (no one likes a whiner).** Any difficulties you're having should be discussed with your support network, who will help you devise a way to make things better.

3. **Start your new position using all the organizing skills you used during your job search—you're guaranteed to get a good start if you approach the job in an organized manner.**

FORTY-TWO STEPS TO A NEW JOB: WHAT YOU NEED TO DO

#1:

I will finish this book by _____. (Set a realistic date.)

#2:

On your calendar, block out time daily to devote to your job search.

#3:

Select a good quality copier paper and
order personalized envelopes to match.

#4:

Order business cards.

#5:

Select a good calendar system with enough space for writing out
appointment information and keeping a daily "to do" list.

#6:

Create a Job Search Notebook.

#7:

Create a set of "Action" files for follow-up.

#8:

Decide how people will reach you and arrange
to have messages taken.

#9:
Make arrangements so that you can both send and receive faxes.

#10:
Fill out worksheet in Chapter 4. Have it completed by _____
(set a date no more than three days from today).

#11:
Research job possibilities by talking to people, looking at job reference material at the library, and visiting sites on the Internet.

#12:
Fill out goal sheets by _____
(this should take no longer than five days).

#13:
Take time to give Exercises 1, 2, and 3 in Chapter 6
careful thought.

#14:
Create a running list of accomplishments.

#15:
Condense your accomplishment list by pairing the career goals
you've set for yourself with the accomplishments
that are relevant to those goals.

#16:

Create a descriptive paragraph that summarizes
appropriate skills and accomplishments.

#17:

Fill out resumé worksheet.

#18:

Prepare a basic cover letter—
one you can adapt each time you need to mail out your resumé.

#19:

Identify people who can serve as your formal or informal mentor(s).
(No need to restrict yourself to one if there are
additional possibilities!)

#20:

Make it a priority to stay active, attend meetings, and circulate
so that you're in touch with people all the time.
You never know who may have the job lead you need.

#21:

Practice making phone calls.

#22:

Practice making eye contact; work on a firm handshake; concentrate on posture; and consider how you speak.

#23:

Ask someone to help you practice being interviewed.

#24:

Start calling to set up informational interviews.

#25:

Conduct as much research on each company as you can before the interview.

#26:

If you would need to relocate for a job, research the community carefully.

#27:

Prepare two interview outfits and have them in your closet and ready to go at all times.

#28:

Keep your briefcase well-organized with basic essentials, including folders for holding extra resumés, literature, and business cards.

#29:
Call ahead to confirm the appointment and to double-check directions and parking.

#30:
Prepare in advance to ease your anxiety and help you feel more in control.

#31:
Write down questions as you think of them in the "Interview Prep" section of your notebook. Note down ideas for your best replies so that you can review them regularly.

AFTER THE INTERVIEW

#32:
Send anything that was requested by the interviewer.

#33:
Make careful notes about what went well and what could have been better.

#34:

Send thoughtful thank-you notes to all whom you met.

#35:

Keep following up.

#36:

Review your notes about the company
so that you can evaluate
the pluses and minuses of the job.

#37:

Evaluate both salary and benefits when you consider
whether or not the compensation for the job is fair.

#38:

When you call back to accept the job, ask for a job offer
letter that puts everything in writing.

#39:

Say thank you to all who helped you
throughout your search.

#40:

Enter into your telephone directory those people
with whom you plan to stay in touch.

#41:

Update your goals sheets and set new goals.

#42:

Stay organized!!

ABOUT THE AUTHORS

RONNI EISENBERG, author of *Organize Yourself!*, has given a multitude of workshops, lectures, and demonstrations across the country on how to get organized. She lives and works in Westport, Connecticut, with her husband and three children.

KATE KELLY, who co-authors Ronni's books, is a professional writer who owns and operates her own publishing business. She lives in Westchester County, New York, with her husband and three children.